PARANORMAL FILES
UFOs

Stuart Webb

ROSEN
PUBLISHING®
New York

This edition published in 2013 by:

The Rosen Publishing Group, Inc.
29 East 21st Street, New York, NY 10010

Editor and Picture Researcher: Joe Harris
U.S. Editor: Bethany Bryan
Design: Jane Hawkins
Cover Design: Jane Hawkins

Library of Congress Cataloging-in-Publication Data

Webb, Stuart.
 UFOs / Stuart Webb. – 1st ed.
    p. cm. – (Paranormal files)
 Includes bibliographical references and index.
 ISBN 978-1-4488-7176-6 (library binding)
 1. Unidentified flying objects–Juvenile literature. I. Title.
 TL789.2.W43 2012
 001.942–dc23
                              2011052522

Manufactured in China

SL002146US

Picture Credits:
Cover: Shutterstock
Interior pages: Corbis: 3, 4, 15, 23, 38, 49. Mary Evans: 6, 11, 13, 16, 20, 72. P. Gray: 49, 70.
Shutterstock: 1, 9, 24, 26, 29, 30, 33, 34, 36, 40, 44, 50, 52, 55, 57, 58, 61, 62, 65, 67, 68, 75.
TopFoto: 18, 43.

CPSIA Compliance Information: Batch #S12YA: For Further Information contact Rosen Publishing, New York, New York at 1-800-237-9932

CONTENTS

THEY CAME FROM OUTER SPACE

The modern UFO phenomenon began with the alleged sighting of "flying saucers" or unidentified flying objects (UFOs) by American pilot Kenneth Arnold in 1947 (see pages 10–15). Many books on the subject describe Arnold's encounter as the first UFO sighting, although it was not recognized as such at the time.

Flying Saucers

Back in 1947, neither Arnold nor anyone else was even thinking about aliens or UFOs. It was assumed that what he had seen was some kind of top-secret military aircraft of revolutionary design. Nor was Arnold's the first sighting of such objects. It was merely the first to make it into the national and international press. For that we must thank the reporter who took Arnold's description of the mysterious aircraft he had seen and dubbed them "flying saucers." The name caught the public imagination and made good newspaper copy.

Many UFOlogists believe that Earth has regularly been visited by aliens since the 1940s.

The story took a dramatic new twist when it became clear that what Arnold believed he had seen did not accord with any secret weapon belonging to the United States. The speed, design, and motion of the aircraft Arnold described were utterly unlike anything being developed at the time. The first thought to spring to the minds of most people in aviation was that the USA's Cold War rival, the Soviet Union, had developed some startling new technology. However, Arnold's aircraft seemed so far in advance of anything the Russians had used during World War II, which had ended only two years earlier, that this seemed rather unlikely.

UFO Files

ARE UFOS REAL?

The witnesses whose stories have been told in this book were probably telling the truth, and believed they really did experience a visitation from another planet. But could their senses have been deceiving them? They might have misidentified astronomical objects such as clouds, planets, bright stars, meteors, artificial satellites, or the moon. A number of UFO reports have been explained by flights of secret aircraft, weapons and weather balloons, or by light phenomena such as mirages and searchlights. Other UFO stories have been the product of deliberate hoaxes. However, there remains a significant percentage of UFO sightings that cannot be explained.

Sightings Multiply

It was not long before people all across the USA started coming forward with their own sightings of mysterious aircraft. It may be that these people had been reluctant to speak publicly before – either because they feared ridicule or because they had not realized that they had seen anything particularly odd. Like Arnold, they may have assumed that they were seeing some secret new type of aircraft. After all, at this time jets, rockets, and helicopters were all new inventions that remained shrouded in mystery. There seemed to be no limit to the inventiveness of aircraft engineers.

At this early stage the reports that were made to the press or the military were usually fairly vague. People reported seeing saucer-shaped objects flying very fast, or bright lights at night moving around in unusual ways. On August 19, 1947, for instance, a Mr. and Mrs. Busby were sitting on the porch of their house in Butte, Montana, with a neighbor, enjoying the warm evening. According to them, a large bright object suddenly flew overhead, heading northeast at a tremendous speed. Ten minutes later, so they claimed, another ten objects came over, flying rather slower, but again heading northeast. According to the startled witnesses, three of the objects peeled off from the triangular formation and headed due north.

Rapid City Sighting

The Busbys did not give any clear description of these objects in terms of size, shape, or color. They merely said that they were bright and moved fast. Somewhat more detailed was the report made by Major Jones of the USAF. Jones was the chief intelligence officer of the 28th Bombardment Wing based at Rapid City Air Force Base in South Dakota. He claimed he was walking across the parking lot at the air base when he saw twelve strange aircraft diving down toward the base from the northwest.

The aircraft were apparently in a tight, diamond- shaped formation, indicating to Jones that they were military aircraft.

He stopped to watch, wondering what type of aircraft these were. When the formation was about 4 miles (6.5 km) away, the aircraft began a slow turn at an altitude of around 5,000 ft (1,500 m). Jones could now see that these strange craft were shaped like elliptical disks and each was about 100 ft (30 m) across. Having turned to face southwest, the craft accelerated to

This artist's impression shows a pair of foo fighters flying alongside a USAF B-24 Liberator bomber over Germany in 1944.

a speed estimated to be around 400 mph (650 kph) and climbed out of sight.

Foo Fighters

It was not only new reports that were surfacing. People were beginning to remember events from previous years that had made no sense at the time, but which now seemed to fit into the flying saucer pattern. Among these were the "foo fighters." These had apparently been seen in large numbers during 1944, and in smaller numbers in 1943 and 1945. They were glowing balls about 3 ft (1 m) across that allegedly flew through the skies over war-torn Europe. The aircrew of Allied bombers claimed to see the foo fighters while on missions over Germany. They were said to fly alongside the bomber formations for several minutes at a time before either disappearing or flying off at high speed.

At first the aircrew believed the foo fighters to be some form of German weapon or tracking system and tried to shoot them down. But bullets seemed to have no effect on them, and since they appeared not to be dangerous, the Allied flyers eventually came to accept them as a feature of the skies over Germany. After the war it was discovered that German pilots had also apparently seen the balls of light accompanying Allied bomber

formations. The Germans had taken the objects to be Allied weapons or devices of some kind. What the foo fighters actually were has never been discovered.

UFO Files

GHOST FLIERS

So-called "ghost fliers" were apparently seen hundreds of times over Finland, Sweden, and Norway between 1932 and 1937. According to witnesses who saw them in daylight, the ghost fliers took the form of extremely large aircraft, bigger than anything then flying, colored gray and without markings of any kind. People who saw them at night claimed that the aircraft often shone dazzlingly bright searchlights down to the ground. The ghost fliers usually came alone, but sometimes appeared in groups of two or three.

At first the various Scandinavian governments thought that they were being spied upon by top-secret scout aircraft from Russia, Germany, or Britain. According to reports, however, the ghost fliers were performing aerobatics and achieving speeds utterly impossible for any known aircraft – and with hindsight impossible even today. Having tried to shoot down the strange intruders, and having spent fruitless days searching for their hidden bases, the Scandinavian authorities lost interest. Reports of sightings faded in 1937 and ceased altogether in 1939 – by which time everyone had more important things on their minds as a world war had begun.

Historic Sightings

UFOs are not just a modern phenomenon. Stories have been told of unexplained objects in the sky throughout history and all over the world. Take, for instance, this report from Japan in 1361: "An object shaped like a drum and about (6 m (20 ft)) in diameter was seen to fly low over the Inland Sea." Another Japanese report, this time from May 1606, records that a "gigantic red wheel" hovered over Nijo Castle in Kyoto for some minutes, then began to spin and flew off.

In 75 bce a Roman priest recorded: "A spark fell from a star and grew larger as it approached the ground to become as large as the moon and as bright as the sun seen through thin clouds. On returning to the sky it took the form of a torch."

On December 5, 1577, a number of "flying objects shaped like hats" that were "black, yellow, and bloody" apparently flew over Germany, and at least one of them, it is claimed, landed temporarily. Given the style of hats at the time, the objects may have been round with a low, domed shape and with a projecting edge or flange around the base – much like today's "flying saucers."

EYEWITNESS ACCOUNT

GREAT BALL OF FIRE

The following account was written by a local government official about an incident that took place in Robozero, Russia, on August 15, 1663, at about 11:30 am. The local peasants were gathered in the church when "a great crash sounded from out of the heavens and many people left the church of God to assemble outside on the square. Now Levka Pedorov (a farmer who dictated this account to the official) was amongst them and saw what happened. To him it was a sign from God. There descended upon Robozero a great ball of fire from the clearest of skies, not from a cloud. Moreover it came from the direction from which we get winter and moved across from the church to the lake. The fire was about 150 ft (45 m) on each side and for the same distance in front of the fire there were two fiery beams. Suddenly it was no longer there, but about one hour of the clock it appeared again, above the lake from which it had disappeared before. It went from the south to the west and was about 1,700 ft (500 m) away when it vanished. But once again it returned, filling all who saw it with a great dread, travelling westwards and staying over Robozero (for) one hour and a half. Now there were fishermen in the boat on the lake about a mile away and they were sorely burnt by the fire. The lake water was lit up to its greatest depths of 30 ft (9 m) and the fish fled to the banks. The water seemed to be covered with rust under the glow."

Is it possible that aliens have been observing the development of human civilization for many centuries?

Different Interpretations

Although the physical descriptions contained in many of these early reports clearly fit what we would today categorize as being UFOs, the witnesses of the time had quite different explanations. In England in 793 CE the sight of blazing objects streaking across the daytime skies over Northumberland was recorded by the local monks as being "dragons."

In September 1235 a Japanese nobleman named Yoritsume saw strange lights in the night sky. The lights were bright, round, and moving in circling or swaying paths to the southwest. Yoritsume summoned the scientific experts of his day, described what he had seen and asked for an explanation. After some days of debate, the scientists came back with the answer that Yoritsume had seen the wind blowing the stars about.

THE UFOs ARRIVE

On the morning of June 24, 1947, Kenneth Arnold, an experienced American aviator, set off from Chehalis, Washington, to his home in Oregon in his single-engine Callier light aircraft. With both time and fuel to spare, he decided first to spend an hour or so over the Mount Rainier area searching for a US military transport aircraft that had been reported missing and was presumed to have crashed. It was while turning on to a new leg of his search pattern at an altitude of 9,200 ft (2,800 m) that Arnold's alleged encounter began. The following is a description of what Arnold claimed happened next…

Arnold's Encounter

A bright flash of light swept over his aircraft. Such a thing usually happened when sun reflected off the surfaces of another aircraft close by. Fearing a collision with an aircraft he had not seen, Arnold hurriedly leveled his plane and scanned the skies, desperately seeking another aircraft. He soon saw a DC4 airliner some miles distant and flying away from him. Discounting this as the source of the flash, he then saw a second flash far to the north.

Staring at the location of the flash, Arnold saw a line of nine aircraft flying towards him at an angle. As the aircraft came closer he saw that they were flying in echelon, a usual military formation, but arranged with the lead aircraft above the others, contrary to the standard military practice. Arnold at this point assumed that the fast-approaching aircraft were military jets of some kind and relaxed. But as the nine aircraft came closer, Arnold was able to see them in detail and at once realized that he was seeing something very strange indeed.

Each aircraft was shaped like a wide crescent with neither fuselage nor tail. Moreover, the aircraft were flying with a strange undulating motion quite unlike the straight-line flight of all known aircraft. They also fluttered or dipped from side to side at times, sending off bright flashes as the sun reflected from their highly polished silver-blue surfaces. There were no markings that Arnold could see, though he was now concentrating hard on the mysterious aircraft. The formation was moving

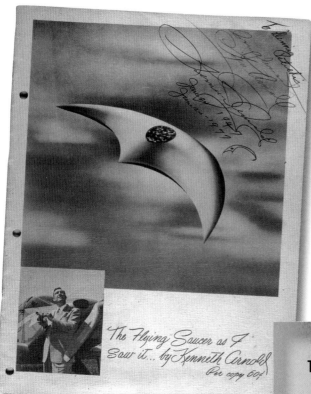

manager of Central Aircraft. The two men discussed the sighting, and Arnold drew pictures of what he had seen. Other pilots and air crew joined the conversation, but none could explain what Arnold had seen, other than to guess that the strange aircraft were some kind of secret military project. Still confused, Arnold then resumed his interrupted flight home to Oregon.

This artwork, signed by Kenneth Arnold, shows the aircraft he claimed to have seen. Arnold himself appears bottom left.

fast. Arnold timed it as it passed over landmarks on the ground and later estimated the speed at around 1,300 mph (2,100 kph). This was much faster than any known aircraft of the time. Even military fast jets flew at only around 700 mph (1,100 kph). The aircraft were soon out of sight.

Secret Military Craft?

Arnold headed for Yakima Airfield and went to see Al Baxter, the general

TALE OF THE PARANORMAL

TWO SHADOWS

Arnold's experience prompted others to come forward with their own stories. A group of boys from Baradine, Australia, were rabbiting by moonlight one night in 1931 when one of them – according to his later report – experienced something very unusual. The first thing he noticed, he said, was that he was casting two shadows. Looking up, he saw a disk-shaped object as bright as the moon approaching from the northwest. Orange lights or flames flashed around its rim and the object rotated slowly as it flew. It followed a straight course before disappearing behind nearby hills.

By the time he arrived home, Arnold had begun to worry that he had seen some sort of highly advanced Soviet war machine. He decided to inform the FBI, but their office was closed, so he dropped in at the offices of the *East Oregonian* newspaper. He told the reporters there all about his experience. One of them, Bill Bequette, queried the way the unusual craft moved. Arnold elaborated on the undulating motion by saying, "They flew like a saucer would if you skipped it across water."

Bequette filed his report with a national news agency, writing about "flying saucers." It was repeated across America and soon the public was agog at news of these flying saucers. Meanwhile, Arnold had returned to the FBI to tell them about the strange aircraft. The local FBI man passed the details on to the head office in Washington, concluding his report with the words, "It is the personal opinion of the interviewer that Arnold actually saw what he states he saw in the attached report." Already concerned about Russian intentions and military technology, the US military pounced on Arnold's report. An era was born.

Eating His Words

News of Arnold's sighting spread quickly through aviation circles, leading to intense speculation. On July 4, 1947, a lunchtime discussion among airline staff at Boise Airport was cut short by

---

TALE OF THE PARANORMAL

SIGHTING AT SNAKE RIVER CANYON

Some of the reports made in the wake of Arnold's sighting were clearly misidentified natural events. A glowing disk-shaped flying object seen over Codroy in Newfoundland turned out to be a meteorite heated red-hot by air friction as it crashed through the atmosphere. Others were harder to explain. For example, Mr. A. C. Urie and his two young sons claimed that on August 15, 1947, they saw a disk flying low over Snake River Canyon in Idaho while they were on a fishing trip. The object, they said, passed them at a distance of just 300 ft (90 m) and though it was moving fast, all three apparently got a good look. It was about 20 ft (6 m), 10 ft (3 m) wide and 10 ft (3 m) high. The object had a flange or rim around its base and made a soft whishing noise as it passed. As it flew out of the canyon, the object traveled low over a line of poplar trees, which bent and twisted as if caught in a sudden, violent wind.

United Airlines pilot E. J. Smith, who declared flatly that it was all nonsense. "I'll believe them when I see them," he finished, slamming down his newspaper and striding off to get his aircraft ready for flight. Smith took off and barely 20 minutes later allegedly found himself confronted by five disk-shaped flying objects, each of which was larger than his own DC3 airliner. The co-pilot and stewardess also claimed to have seen the objects before they flew off at high speed.

The Roswell Incident

Just two weeks after Arnold's sighting, the press officer, Walter Haut, at Roswell Air Force Base in New Mexico issued a dramatic press release. He said a flying saucer had crashed near the base and that air force personnel were investigating the debris. The press pounced on the story, expecting that the mystery of the flying saucers would soon be solved. Later that same day, however, a rather embarrassed Major Jesse Marcel called a press conference to announce that the crashed flying saucer was, in fact, a weather balloon of a new type that the Roswell men had not recognized.

Fate *magazine, launched in 1948, led its first edition with the Arnold sighting.*

Like a Flash Gordon Rocket Ship

More typical of the early reports of flying saucers was one made by Eastern Airlines pilots Clarence Chiles and John Whitted. They claimed that on the night of July 23, 1948, they were flying a DC3 passenger flight over Alabama when they saw what they took to be another aircraft some distance ahead of them. Within seconds Chiles and Whitted realized that the other aircraft was coming toward them at great speed. They braced themselves to take emergency evasive action to avoid a collision, but the object passed them at a distance of a few hundred feet, then shot away to vanish into the distance behind them.

According to the pilots, the mystery aircraft had been in sight for only a few seconds, but had come very close and both men were confident that they had got a good look at it. They reported that the object was shaped like a rocket or cigar and that it glowed pale blue over its entire surface with a brightness that hurt their eyes when it was at its closest. There was a row of what might have been windows along the center of the craft's side. There were small flames or fumes coming from the rear of the object. Whitted later described what he had seen as like "a Flash Gordon rocket ship."

The Mantell Incident

An incident with far more serious consequences took place at Godman Air Force Base in Virginia on January 7, 1948. At lunchtime that day, guards at the nearby Fort Knox army post phoned the control tower at Godman to report that a large, unidentified object had been seen in the sky heading toward the air base. Colonel Guy Hix, commander at Godman, was alerted and he sprinted to the control tower just in time to see, so he later claimed, a large, reddish object fly overhead.

The sky was dotted with clouds and nobody had enjoyed a good view of the object. Hix was not an officer to take chances, however. Something had intruded into the air space that it was his duty to guard, and it had to be investigated. Hix scrambled the three P-51 fighter aircraft that were kept on standby at the base. The aircraft took off and set out in pursuit of the mysterious object.

Giving Chase

Flight Commander Captain Thomas Mantell sighted the object first as the three aircraft emerged from the clouds. The other two pilots radioed to say that they could see the object and Mantell's aircraft giving chase. But cloud closed in again, and they lost sight of the object and Mantell. After searching for a while they turned back to Godman.

Mantell, meanwhile, was in hot pursuit. He sent three radio messages with updates on his progress, then nothing. After several minutes of radio silence from Mantell, Hix began to worry. Calls were put out, but Mantell did not respond. More aircraft were scrambled to search the skies for the mysterious object and for Mantell's P-51. The aircraft went up as high as 33,000 ft (10,000 m) and spread out for 100 miles (160 km), but they saw nothing.

EYEWITNESS ACCOUNT

MANTELL'S FINAL RADIO MESSAGES

"I've sighted the thing. It looks metallic and it's tremendous in size."

A few minutes later: "The thing's starting to climb. It's making half my speed. I'll try to close in."

Last message, ten minutes after his comrades lost sight of him: "It is still above me, making my speed or better. I'm going up to 20,000 feet (6,000 m). If I'm no closer then, I'll abandon the chase."

Three fighter jets were scrambled to intercept the UFO over Kentucky.

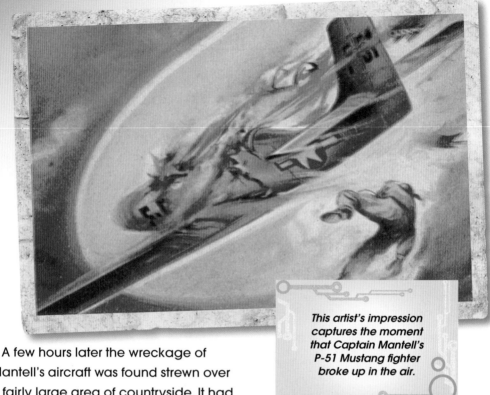

This artist's impression captures the moment that Captain Mantell's P-51 Mustang fighter broke up in the air.

A few hours later the wreckage of Mantell's aircraft was found strewn over a fairly large area of countryside. It had obviously broken up at high altitude and fallen to the ground in thousands of pieces.

Project Sign

The death of Mantell turned the UFO phenomenon into an issue of deadly seriousness. It seemed unlikely that the USAF would allow its pilots to chase after one of their own secret weapons, and equally unlikely that the Soviet Union would risk testing secret aircraft in US airspace. So what did Mantell and his fellow pilots chase that day?

USAF set up Project Sign to get to the bottom of the mystery. This was an investigative team of air force officers and civilian experts whose job was

to analyze all known reports of flying saucers and produce a final and definitive answer. Among the civilian experts recruited to Project Sign was Dr. J. Allen Hynek. An astronomer of great repute, Hynek's task was to see if any of the reports could be explained as being meteors, comets, or stars seen under unusual conditions.

Project Sign investigated 237 sightings, selecting them on the grounds of witness credibility and detail of observation. After a year of work, Sign concluded that 77 percent of these reports could be explained as comets, stars, conventional aircraft, weather balloons, or other perfectly normal things seen under unusual or misleading circumstances. The remaining 23 percent were labeled as "Unknown explanation."

The Grudge Report

Project Sign's report was deemed too sensitive for public consumption, so another, edited version, known as the Grudge Report, was released in December 1949. The Grudge Report played down the results, and recommended that the USAF cease detailed investigations of flying saucers. This may seem odd, with 23 percent of reports being classified as "unknown," but from the viewpoint of the USAF, it made perfect sense.

The task of the air force was not, and is not, to investigate strange phenomena, no matter how interesting they might be. Its task is to protect the USA and its allies from air attack. By 1949 the Cold War with the Soviet Union was becoming serious. The Soviet Union had many hundreds of jet fighters and jet bombers, plus an unknown number of rocket-powered missiles for the USAF to worry about.

From Flying Saucers to UFOs

The press and the public had not lost interest, however. Reports continued to be filed and were featured by the press and broadcast media. Some reporters took a particular interest in flying saucers, as did some air professionals and members of the public. Since it was now becoming clear that only some of the reported craft were disk-shaped – Arnold's originals had been crescent-shaped – the popular name of flying saucers was gradually replaced by a new term: unidentified flying object (UFO). This was thought to lend an air of scientific rigor to the study, and implied that the investigators were not prejudging the eventual solution to the riddle.

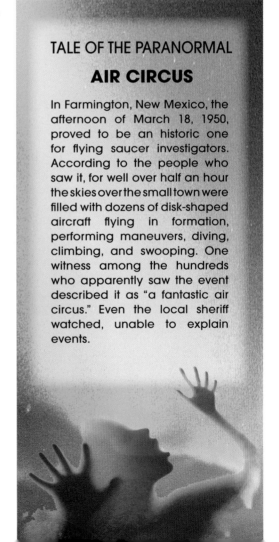

TALE OF THE PARANORMAL

AIR CIRCUS

In Farmington, New Mexico, the afternoon of March 18, 1950, proved to be an historic one for flying saucer investigators. According to the people who saw it, for well over half an hour the skies over the small town were filled with dozens of disk-shaped aircraft flying in formation, performing maneuvers, diving, climbing, and swooping. One witness among the hundreds who apparently saw the event described it as "a fantastic air circus." Even the local sheriff watched, unable to explain events.

Astronomers Get in on the Act

It was not only aviators who were encountering flying saucers. On August 20, 1949, no less a figure than Clyde Tombaugh, the astronomer who had discovered Pluto, got involved in the growing mystery of flying saucers. At 10:45 pm he was sitting outside his house at Las Cruces, New Mexico, with his wife and her mother. His eye was caught, so he later said, by a green light flying overhead. According to Tombaugh, he looked up and saw seven other lights, all of the same green color and all flying a parallel course. He thought that he could just make out a dark shape behind the lights, as if they were windows or lights attached to a large, unlit aircraft, but he could not be certain. The craft made no sound as it powered overhead and vanished into the distance.

On May 20 the following year, another astronomer saw a flying saucer. This was Dr. Seymour Hess of the Lowell Observatory at Flagstaff, Arizona. So Hess said, he was outside the

The astronomer Clyde Tombaugh sights eight mysterious green lights in the sky over his house in the Arizona desert in 1949.

observatory checking cloud cover when he spotted a bright object in the sky. He studied it through his binoculars for some seconds as it flew past. He later described the object as a shiny disk that was flying through thin cloud, sometimes disappearing behind the cloud and at other times flying beneath it. After a few seconds, the object flew out of sight.

Dogfight off Long Island

On October 29, 1952, two F94 jet fighters were patrolling off Long Island, New York. The F94 was not only heavily armed and fast, but had air-to-air radar operated by a second crew member sitting behind the pilot. The two aircraft were piloted by Lieutenant Burt Deane and Lieutenant Ralph Corbett. According to Deane, at about 2 am he saw a bright white light ahead of the jets at an estimated 8 miles (13 km) distance. The following account is based on their own description of what happened next.

Aware that they were the first fast fighters to get this close to a flying saucer, Deane and Corbett decided to attack. Corbett got a radar lock first, but it was Deane who pushed his fighter to full power to close in for the attack. At once, the UFO began to move quickly, cutting inside the curve of Deane's turn. Deane pulled his fighter into its

tightest possible turn, almost blacking out due to the extreme g-force, but he could not match the performance of the mystery aircraft. Corbett now came up to the attack, using standard fighter tactics to try to push the UFO into range of Deane's guns. It was to no avail. Whatever the pilots tried, the UFO managed to slip aside at the last moment – often at speeds or performing turns quite impossible for the pursuing F94 fighters.

After about 10 minutes of dogfighting, the UFO climbed steeply away at supersonic speed. Deane and Corbett gave chase but were rapidly outpaced. The investigators who questioned the two pilots about the incident put it down as "unexplained."

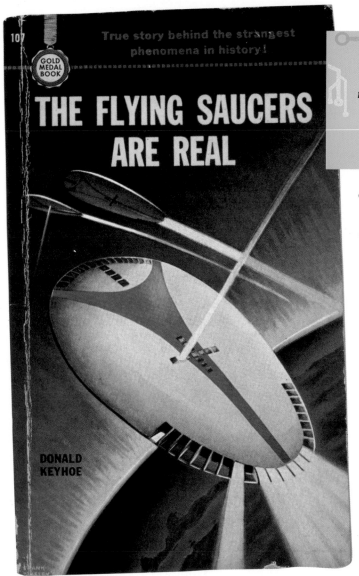

True story behind the strangest phenomena in history!

GOLD MEDAL BOOK

THE FLYING SAUCERS ARE REAL

DONALD KEYHOE

In this seminal book, Major Donald Keyhoe advanced the theory that flying saucers were alien spacecraft, and the US military was covering up the truth.

access to any of the secret reports, he did learn of their existence. Keyhoe gradually came to a series of startling conclusions, which he published in his classic 1950 book *The Flying Saucers Are Real*.

Donald Keyhoe theorized that Earth had been under observation by beings from another planet, or series of planets, for some 200 years or more. He believed that the sudden upsurge in sightings after 1947 was linked to the detonation of the first atomic bomb in 1945. Keyhoe argued that the invention of

Donald Keyhoe

One man who was determined to get to the bottom of the mystery was retired US Marines officer Major Donald Keyhoe. Keyhoe had extensive personal contacts within the military, which enabled him to talk to many witnesses firsthand and to see many written reports. Although he was denied

atomic power was a key moment in the progress of a civilization and that any more advanced culture would be bound to take notice of the crossing of this threshold.

The increased sightings of flying saucers were, Keyhoe argued, evidence that the previously sporadic observation of humanity by aliens

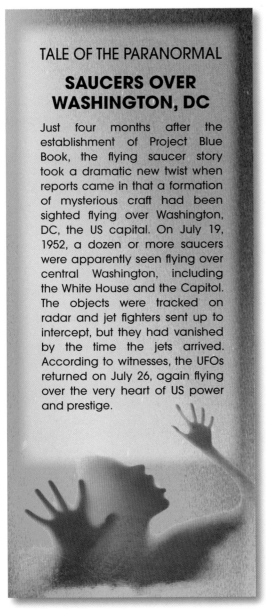

TALE OF THE PARANORMAL

SAUCERS OVER WASHINGTON, DC

Just four months after the establishment of Project Blue Book, the flying saucer story took a dramatic new twist when reports came in that a formation of mysterious craft had been sighted flying over Washington, DC, the US capital. On July 19, 1952, a dozen or more saucers were apparently seen flying over central Washington, including the White House and the Capitol. The objects were tracked on radar and jet fighters sent up to intercept, but they had vanished by the time the jets arrived. According to witnesses, the UFOs returned on July 26, again flying over the very heart of US power and prestige.

had been stepped up. In due course, Keyhoe argued, the aliens would make contact – though when, where, or how would be up to them. In his book he revealed that the Grudge Report had been the public façade for a top-secret

report. But he asserted, wrongly, that the secret report had concluded that the flying saucers were, in fact, alien spaceships. He further alleged that this conclusion had been suppressed in the Grudge Report because the authorities feared that it would cause a public panic.

Keyhoe's book was an immediate success. It was reprinted just two weeks after being published and eventually sold over half a million copies. By the autumn of 1950 the idea that flying saucers were alien spacecraft had taken a firm hold of the public imagination and was assumed as fact in most press reports of UFOs.

Project Blue Book

The USAF eventually decided that the continuing flow of eyewitness reports of UFOs demanded some sort of response. In March 1952, Captain Edward J. Ruppelt was put in charge of the Air Technical Intelligence Center (ATIC), the organization tasked with collecting and analyzing UFO reports. Ruppelt was given neither orders nor resources to investigate reports or theories – the USAF believed that task had been completed with the Grudge Report. Ruppelt turned to various officers and others, such as Dr. J. Allen Hynek, with an interest in the subject and persuaded several to work part-time or without pay on the new initiative. Ruppelt's task was given the code name Project Blue Book.

The Robertson Panel

The dramatic sightings over Washington (see panel on page 21) not only put flying saucers back at the top of the news agenda, but also created a widespread alarm that aliens were about to invade. Hundreds of reports of new sightings of disks and other flying objects poured into the USAF. These overwhelmed not just Project Blue Book, but most of the USAF's reporting systems designed to watch for intruding enemy aircraft and missiles. The CIA became worried that if a Soviet missile attack really did happen, it might be mistaken for a UFO sighting. It therefore decided that the best action was to persuade the American public that flying saucers simply did not exist.

To this end it persuaded Dr. H. P. Robertson, a respected physicist, to convene a panel of scientists who would study saucer reports and lay to rest the rumor that they were alien spacecraft. The Robertson Panel duly reported in January 1953, concluding that unidentified flying objects were just that – quite normal, innocent objects that, for one reason or other, had been misidentified by those who saw them.

In 1969 the USAF announced that "the continuation of Project Blue Book cannot be justified either on the grounds of national security or in the interest of science." Project Blue Book was closed down. Officially the US government has had no further interest in the UFO or alien issue. Many people suspect that it has maintained a very active unofficial interest, but if this is true, the government has shrouded the issue in mystery and secrecy.

TALE OF THE PARANORMAL

NEAR COLLISION OVER LAREDO

On December 4, 1952, over Laredo in Texas, a USAF officer named Earl Fogle was on a night patrol in the direction of the Mexican border. According to Fogle, during the course of his patrol he saw a blue, round object flying some distance away. The object, Fogle later said, changed direction to intercept his F51 fighter. It then turned onto a collision course and approached at high speed. At the last moment the object turned aside, climbed steeply then came down for a second pass. This being peacetime, Fogle had been flying with his lights on. He now turned them off and dived rapidly away from the approaching object. Glancing over his shoulder, Fogle saw the blue object circle as if looking for him, then it climbed away and vanished from sight.

A Cover-Up?

The US government's policy of outright denial bred distrust and hostility among those who were investigating the phenomenon, and encouraged the spread of conspiracy theories. Some suspect that behind the dismissive attitudes of the Grudge Report and the Robertson Panel there lurked a darker and more ominous reality. They argue that if the US government did in fact know that UFOs were alien spacecraft, and perhaps had even captured one, it would naturally seek to deny the fact so that it could keep its discoveries secret – either to avoid public panic, or to prevent enemy governments from learning these secrets for themselves. According to this theory, all government activity and pronouncements on the issue have been motivated by a desire to cover up the truth.

Since 1953, most governments, following the US lead, have either denied that UFOs exist or refused to comment on the subject. Meanwhile, members of the public have continued to report strange, bizarre, and sometimes terrifying sights in the sky. It has been left to part-time amateur investigators to try to make sense of what is happening.

A group of USAF technical officers meet in 1952 to review the evidence relating to UFOs. Captain Edward J. Ruppelt is standing third from left.

CLOSE ENCOUNTERS

On March 6, 1957, at about 2 pm, a woman in Trenton, New Jersey, was clearing up her back room when she heard her dog barking in the backyard. According to her later statement, she went out to see what was causing the fuss and saw the dog barking excitedly and looking up at a round flying object. Thus far, this represents a standard UFO sighting. What made it more valuable to UFO researchers was the fact that the alleged object was seen in broad daylight at close quarters, enabling the woman to make a detailed description of the UFO and its movements. This type of sighting would later come to be classified as a "close encounter of the first kind," or CE1 (see panel).

UFOs are consistently described by witnesses as having a disk shape, with a central raised dome.

Immediately after the sighting, the woman phoned her husband, who was at work in New York. He advised her to write down an account of her experience while it was still fresh in her mind. This she did, describing it as follows: the object was some 500 ft (150 m) away and about 50 ft (15 m) across. She likened its shape to that of a derby or bowler hat. The central domed area was about 30 ft (9 m) high with steep sides while the flat bottom extended beyond the dome to form a rim about 15 ft (5 m) wide. The color and texture of the object was that of pipe clay, a smooth but dull off-white substance. As the woman watched, the object began to rock or sway slightly from side to side. A low rumbling noise began that grew louder, then faded only to become louder again. There then came a soft whooshing noise and the object rose vertically to disappear into the clouds.

The woman sent her account to the USAF, where it was quietly filed away in Project Blue Book. Her account bore similarities to many other reports of sightings in terms of the shape of the object and its wobbling or rocking motion.

UFO Files

CLASSIFYING UFO SIGHTINGS

In 1972, Dr. J. Allen Hynek (see page 16) devised a classification system for UFO sightings. The system comprises so-called "encounters" (UFOs seen at a distance) and "close encounters." A "close encounter of the first kind" (CE1) is when a UFO is seen at close quarters and for a fairly prolonged period of time. The witness is able to give a detailed description of the UFO, its shape, color, and behavior.

A "close encounter of the second kind" (CE2) is essentially similar to a CE1, but where the UFO has some clear impact on its surroundings. This might be as simple as causing vegetation to sway as it passes, or may involve burning plants or ground with what appear to be engine blasts. A key feature is that the effect must be unique. To take an example, if a UFO is seen to land and marks are afterward found where the UFO rested, these marks should be unique and not identical to marks left by farm machinery nearby. Some UFO investigators collect samples of burnt grass and disturbed soil in the hope that analysis may reveal something about the motive power or composition of the UFO that affected them.

A "close encounter of the third kind" (CE3) occurs when a CE1 or CE2 is combined with the appearance of what seem to be occupants or crew from the UFO. In this book, we shall be focusing on CE1s and CE2s.

Photographic Evidence

Another CE1 took place in January 1958 when a Brazilian survey ship, the *Almirante Saldanha*, arrived at the Brazilian naval base on the Pacific island of Trinidade. Just after noon on the 16th the photographer Almiro Barauna was on deck when, it is claimed, another crew member pointed out to him an object in the sky. Barauna at first took the object to be an aircraft, but its lack of wings made him reach for his camera. The object circled around the island, then flew off. Before it did so, Barauna managed to take four photos.

The Trinidade sighting is famous largely because of the photos that were taken. The UFO shows features that are commonly mentioned in reports of sightings. The shape of a flattened sphere with a rim is one that crops up in a great many cases. That apart, the behavior of the UFO was not particularly noteworthy. It apparently flew at a speed easily attained by conventional aircraft and its flight path, circling the island and heading off in a straight line, could be mimicked by a

This is one of the famous photos taken by Almiro Barauna of a "UFO" sighted from the Brazilian ship Almirante Saldanha in 1958.

human craft. Were it not for the photos, skeptics might have dismissed this sighting as that of a misidentified aircraft.

Realizing that there must be no suspicion of fraud or hoaxing, Barauna persuaded the captain of the ship to supervise the developing of the photos in the on-board laboratory, and on the ship's return to port he submitted the negatives and prints to the Brazilian navy for expert study.

In his excitement, Barauna had not checked the settings on the camera and all four pictures were consequently slightly over-exposed. Nevertheless, the craft was recognizable as being a flattened sphere with a wide rim or flange around its center, giving a rather Saturn-like appearance. The body of the craft was pale gray, the rim dark gray and a greenish mist or spray trailed behind it. The overall diameter of the craft was estimated to be 130 ft (40 m), and its speed around 600 mph (950 kph).

About a hundred sailors and residents at the base also apparently saw the UFO, and the developed photos matched exactly the descriptions given by several of these witnesses.

Chase Over Portage County

On the night of April 16, 1966, Deputy Sheriffs Dale Spaur and Wilbur Neff were out on patrol in Portage County, Ohio. They were driving along Route 224 when they saw an abandoned wrecked car by the roadside and stopped to investigate. While Neff waited beside the police car, Spaur walked over to the wreck. Spaur inspected the car, concluded that nobody was around, and turned to go back to the police car. The following is based on descriptions by Spaur, Neff, and other witnesses of what happened next...

TALE OF THE PARANORMAL

SPINNING DISK

In 1980 bus conductor Russel Callaghan was on his usual route through the Yorkshire countryside near Bradford. Having reached the end of the journey, Callaghan and his driver halted the bus for a few minutes before the return trip. As they sat having a conversation on the grass the two men allegedly spotted a silver disk hovering over Emley Moor about 650 ft (200 m) away. The disk, they later said, began to spin, gaining speed and then began to move. It gathered speed quickly and streaked out of view in about eight seconds.

Spaur claimed he saw a large, brightly lit object coming toward them. He told Neff to turn around, which he did before freezing in alarm. The object was getting closer, and could now be seen to be about 40 ft (12 m) tall. It was emitting a quiet humming sound. The glowing object pulsated with various colors bright enough to light up the surrounding area. It was shaped like a football standing upright, though the top was more rounded and domed than the more pointed bottom. The object hovered over the police car for a few minutes at a height of about 800 ft (250 m), then moved off east. Spaur and Neff gave chase in their car.

They were later joined by Officer Wayne Huston, who was parked up on Route 14 when the UFO came flashing past, chased by Spaur and Neff. The object halted again near the village of Harmony. The three policemen stopped and got out of their cars to watch the UFO as it hung in the air, then climbed up at speed and disappeared from view. Before it disappeared, the object was also allegedly seen by a fourth policeman, Patrolman Frank Panzanella.

The key point about the Portage County sighting is that the object was seen at close quarters and from various angles over a considerable period of time by four different witnesses.

EYEWITNESS ACCOUNT

FRANK PANZANELLA'S STORY

I saw 2 other patrol cars pull up and the officers (Neff, Spaur, and Huston) got out of the car (sic) and asked me if I saw it. I replyed (sic) SAW WHAT! Then pointed at the object and I told them that I had been watching it for the last 10 minutes. The object was the shape of a half of (a) football, was very bright, and was about 25 to 35 ft (8–11 m) in diameter. The object then moved out towards Harmony Township approximately 1,000 feet high (300 m), then it stopped then went straight up real fast to about 3,500 ft (1,070 m).

Encounter in Western Australia

Australian farmer A. Pool was driving back to his farm after a long day tending sheep on his station in Western Australia. Pool was trundling across a grassy paddock in his off-road vehicle when he spotted an aircraft about 2,625 ft (800 m) away heading toward him. Thinking a pilot was in trouble, he braked to a halt to await events. According to Pool, the approaching aircraft turned out to be a gray-colored disk flying at about 400 ft (120 m) above the ground and heading downward. When he switched off his engine, he heard a loud whine similar to an electric motor running at high speed, coming from what he now realized was no ordinary aircraft.

The object continued to dive until it came to a halt, hovering about 6 ft (2 m) from the ground and barely 10 ft (3 m) from Pool's car. He sat staring at the object, noticing that it had a flat underside and domed topside. The object was some 20 ft (6 m) across and at one end had a sort of upward bulge, which Pool took to be a cabin. There was what seemed to be a window on one side, but he could not see through it.

Close encounters always seem to take place in remote places, far from cities and other places where large crowds gather.

After sitting in amazement for some seconds, Pool decided to get out of his car and approach the strange object. No sooner had he opened the door, however, than the disk rocked to one side, then shot off at high speed.

UFO Sightings in Communist Countries

Throughout the 1950s, 1960s, and 1970s, reports of UFO sightings came largely from North America and Europe. Critics argued that this was because the initial flying saucer stories that originated with the Kenneth Arnold sighting (see pages 4–5, 10–12, 13) had been publicized in those areas, prompting people to misreport normal objects. But gradually reports of sightings began to come from other parts of the world.

It later transpired that UFO sightings had been reported regularly over the Soviet Union (primarily in modern-day Russia) and other communist countries from 1947 onward. However the authorities there had imposed a news blackout on the subject. However, news of these sightings did begin to leak out during the 1960s. Some of these reports dated back to the late 1940s and early 1950s, just when UFOs had begun to be seen in numbers over the USA and Europe.

The reports were mostly secondhand and included few details. Typical of the early reports is one from the Polish city of Poznan in 1957. A local newspaper reported on January 31 that an unknown aircraft shaped like a disk had been seen flying

Could the solitary UFOs seen by witnesses today be the advance scouts of an interplanetary invasion force?

overhead, but gave no other details.
Later reports tended to be more helpful.

Sighting in Czechoslovakia

On the warm evening of July 1, 1966,
Vlasta Rosenauerova was sitting on
the veranda of her house near Pilzen,
Czechoslovakia (in what is now
the Czech Republic), while her two
grandchildren played nearby. Mrs.
Rosenauerova said later that she was
about to call the children in when
she saw two lights approaching from
the north. They were diving as they
approached, she said, and had a
yellowish-red color similar to that of a
candle flame. When the objects were
an estimated 1.25 miles (2 km) distant,
one stopped, followed by the other.

Mrs. Rosenauerova described the
two objects as being identical in
size and shape. Each was spherical
with a domed bulge on top and
was about 115 ft (35 m) across. Mrs.
Rosenauerova pointed the lights out
to her grandchildren, whereupon the
younger one, a boy, burst into tears.
As Mrs. Rosenauerova comforted her
grandson, the elder child, a girl of
about nine years of age, called out,
"Look, Grandma, it is on fire." The left
hand object was indeed spouting what
seemed to be a thin column of smoke.
A few seconds later both objects
changed color to bright white and
accelerated away to the northeast until
they were out of sight.

TALE OF THE PARANORMAL

INCIDENTS IN HUNGARY AND YUGOSLAVIA

On November 20, 1967, the
Hungarian poet Laszlo Benjamin
and a friend, Peter Kuczka, were
walking down Krisztina Avenue in
Budapest when a large aircraft
flew low overhead. According to
Benjamin, when he glanced up he
saw not the passenger aircraft he
expected but a spherical object
about 70 ft (21 m) across, with a thin
flange or rim around its middle. The
object gave out a bright white flash
of light, then took off at high speed.

Three days later a Yugoslavian
Communist Party official named
Punisja Vuiovici described his own
encounter. He said he was passing
the shores of Lake Krupat when
he saw what he initially took to be
a shooting star. As he watched,
however, the object came right
down to hover over the water while
emitting a pulsating white light
brighter than any star. The object was
conical in shape, though Vuiovici did
not hazard a guess as to its size. After
a few seconds it flew off.

Romanian Story

On September 21, 1968, Nicolae Radulescu, an engineer in Romania's Ploesti oil fields, was watching a brilliant sunset from his apartment window when, he later claimed, he saw an object flying past. It was, he said, colored pale red or pink and shaped like a disk, though its precise shape was unclear due to it being surrounded by a mist or spray of gas. The object flew northward with an undulating motion for about five seconds, then turned abruptly and shot off to the west.

Cigar-Shaped UFOs

Although the vast majority of UFO sightings are of spherical or disk-shaped objects, not all fit this pattern. A good number of UFOs are reported to be shaped like a cigar. On May 6, 1952, farmer R. Geppart was ploughing a wheat field near Wagga Wagga in New South Wales, Australia, in the cool of dawn when he saw lights approaching.

At first Geppart took little notice, taking the lights to be the headlights of a car on the road, but as they got closer he realized there was something odd about them. According to Geppart, the lights were in the air and not on the road and they were fixed to a larger object that glowed faintly. The object, he said, was about 100 ft (30 m) long and 20 ft (6 m) across. It was moving more slowly than an aircraft and at a height of some 250 ft (75 m).

It passed Geppart at a distance of just 400 ft (120 m), so he got a good look. There was a reddish nose cone and behind that what Geppart took to be round windows or portholes through which light was streaming from inside the object – these being the lights that had first attracted his attention. The object glided past in absolute silence, then picked up speed and vanished into the distance.

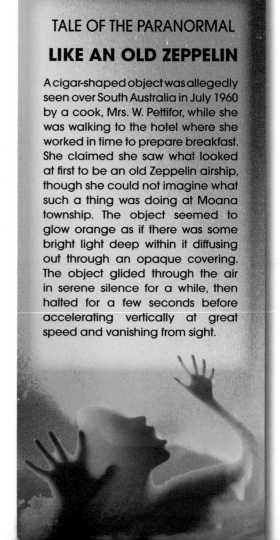

TALE OF THE PARANORMAL

LIKE AN OLD ZEPPELIN

A cigar-shaped object was allegedly seen over South Australia in July 1960 by a cook, Mrs. W. Pettifor, while she was walking to the hotel where she worked in time to prepare breakfast. She claimed she saw what looked at first to be an old Zeppelin airship, though she could not imagine what such a thing was doing at Moana township. The object seemed to glow orange as if there was some bright light deep within it diffusing out through an opaque covering. The object glided through the air in serene silence for a while, then halted for a few seconds before accelerating vertically at great speed and vanishing from sight.

Cigar-shaped UFOs are the second most reported variety, after the classic disk-shaped UFO.

The Warminster Flap

Very often sightings are single events that come and go without warning. But sometimes there occur what have become known as flaps – when several sightings take place within a fairly small area over a reasonably short period of time. One of the most famous such flaps began on April 1, 1965, in the rather mundane surroundings of a council car park in Warminster, a small market town in Wiltshire, England.

Charles Hudd, an employee of Warminster Council, was reporting for work at 4:45 am when he claims he spotted a large silver object flying through the sky. The object, according to Hudd, was rectangular in shape, rounded at both ends, and moved in total silence. Hudd called the attention of three workmates to the object and all four men watched as it moved off to hover over Cop Heap, a nearby hill. As it hovered the silver object gradually turned red, then abruptly split open and turned into four smaller red balls that dropped toward the ground before streaking off to the north.

The Silver Object Returns

Given the date, the local newspaper editor was not inclined to believe Hudd when the report came in. Though he did not print it, he filed it for future use. That use was not long in coming. Three days later, a bank manager claimed he sighted what seemed to be the same silver object 2 miles (3 km) south of Warminster as he drove home after working late. The silver object this time remained intact, but he said it was followed by four orange balls as it cruised south over Cradle Hill.

In the early hours of April 7 two army officers, Lieutenants R. Ashwood and P. Davies of the Welch Regiment were

If UFOs are of alien origin, as many believe, they have crossed vast distances, measured in light years, to reach Earth.

leaving a particularly good dinner in Warminster when they allegedly spotted a silver disk flying overhead at high speed. The object flashed over the town, swept over Cradle Hill, and vanished into the distance.

The Thing

The trio of sightings in one week caused a sensation in the town. The "Thing," as the phenomenon was known locally, prompted many local people to come forward to report odd noises they had heard in the weeks leading up to the sightings. At the time they had assumed the noises were being made by the army at their exercise grounds on nearby Salisbury Plain, but now people were not so sure.

At 9 pm on June 3 the Thing was back. This time, according to reports, the silver, cigar-shaped object glowed brightly in the night sky as it hovered over Heytesbury, a village south of Warminster. The witnesses were the wife and children of the local vicar. Twelve-year-old Nigel Phillips had a small telescope, which he excitedly trained on the object. With its aid he saw a protrusion toward one end of the object that was more orange than silver. The boy drew a picture. It was that picture that catapulted the Warminster Thing into the national media.

Cradle Hill Sightings

Journalists hurried to Warminster to gather stories. Reports of disks and cigar-shaped objects in the sky over Warminster continued to come in during June, July, and August. Many of these seemed centered around Cradle Hill.

On August 10 truck driver Terry Pell of Lincolnshire was driving a load of vegetables from his home county to a storage depot at Warminster. As he came down Cop Heap Lane at around 4:30 am, he claims he saw a 30 ft (9 m) diameter ball of crimson flame tumbling down the slopes of Cradle Hill.

EYEWITNESS ACCOUNT

STRANGE SOUNDS

At 11 pm on the 28th of March, 1965, Eric Payne was walking down a dark, foggy, quiet country road near Warminster when he heard a sound he described as similar to the sound of the wind in telegraph wires. The sound increased in intensity, however, and he was pushed and held down by "a tremendous racket ... (like) ... a gigantic tin can with huge nuts and bolts inside it, rattling over your head." He heard a shrill whining and buzzing that "nearly drove me mad." He reports that his "head was pushed from side to side and I might as well have left my arms and legs at home for all the use they were. I simply could not stop this tremendous downward pressure. I crawled round in the road for a bit and then sank to my knees on the grass verge."

This artist's impression shows the triangular craft that witnesses reported seeing in the Wiltshire sky on January 14, 1966.

As Pell watched, the ball apparently gathered speed, then changed direction and came straight toward him. Pell reported that he slammed his brakes on, then swerved to avoid a collision with the great ball of fire. The truck ended up in a fence and the badly shaken Pell watched the fireball climb rapidly and then vanish.

Peter Wilsher and his fiancée Ann claimed they spotted four silver disks circling Cradle Hill on August 25, 1965. The disks were in view for several minutes and they changed color from silver to pale red before flying off. The couple were on holiday from Essex and had missed the fuss about the Thing. When Wilsher mentioned the sighting in a local pub, he didn't expect to be taken seriously, but was pounced on by locals who demanded details and then sent him to see the editor of the local newspaper.

On August 27, a public meeting was arranged in the town hall to which hundreds turned up, and hundreds more had to be turned away. Little was achieved, except that dozens of people recounted their sightings and a government official stated that the Thing was not some secret army weapon that was out of control.

Final Flurry

Thereafter, sightings of the Thing tailed off for a while, before a final, brief flurry of activity around the turn of the year. On the morning of December 20 Eva Robinson said she saw a silver cigar-shaped object flying over the hills outside town as she walked to work. On January 4, 1966, Rosemary Bell reported a gleaming orange ball rolling through the sky. Some teenagers claimed that on January 14 they saw a strange, gold-colored, triangular-shaped craft pass overhead at the village of Battlesbury. A group of children playing in fields three nights later said they saw a chain of white lights flash overhead.

By this time the Warminster flap had become national and international news. The focus of sightings around Cradle Hill led one group of young UFO enthusiasts to set up a nightly watch on the summit of the hill. The watch lasted for months, but not much was seen. As with other flaps elsewhere, the one at Warminster seemed to peter out inconclusively.

UFO Files

FLAP PATTERNS

Some UFO researchers (UFOlogists) have noticed that there tends to be a pattern to flaps. Initially, there are a number of sightings of UFOs, which built rapidly to a peak, with a large number of sightings being made in the space of a few days or couple of weeks. Thereafter the number of sightings declines in both number and quality as CE1s are replaced by more distant encounters. Then, after a final brief spate of sightings, the flap ends and quiet returns. Why should this be? UFOlogists have speculated that the pattern has more to do with how people react to a flap than to the flap itself. They hold that the initial large number of high-quality sightings is evidence of intense UFO activity. This is then reported in the media. In the weeks that follow, people report as UFOs things that they might otherwise not have thought unusual or that could be adequately explained as normal events and objects. The final blip may be due either to a return of real UFO activity or to a review of the story by the media. Thus, according to his point of view, what might be only a few days of real UFO activity gets stretched out into an apparent flap lasting many months.

The Exeter Incident

The Exeter incident, as it became known, gained fame largely because the two policemen involved refused to accept the dismissive "official explanations" issued by Project Blue Book. The incident, which took place near the town of Exeter, New Hampshire, began at 1 am on September 3, 1965. Patrolman Eugene Bertrand was driving along Route 108 when he saw a car parked by the side of the road in a remote rural spot and pulled over to investigate. Inside the car Bertrand found a woman driver in a state of some distress. She said that her car had been followed by a bright white light in the sky that had dived down to hover over the vehicle. She had then stopped

Were the bright lights that Muscarello saw in fact alien spacecraft?

and the light flew off as Bertrand approached. After a quarter of an hour the light had not returned, so the woman drove off while Bertrand continued his patrol.

Bertrand reported back to Exeter Police Station at about 2:30 am. There he found Norman Muscarello who was shaking with fear and almost unable to talk. After a few minutes, Bertrand and desk sergeant Reginald Towland managed to calm Muscarello down and get his story from him. Muscarello said he had been hitchhiking on Route 150 and had been unable to get a lift, so he was walking to Exeter. He had reached Carl Dining Field Farm when, he claimed, a group of five red lights came swooping down from the sky to hover over a house about 100 ft (30 m) from where Muscarello was standing. The red lights began to pulsate in a pattern that repeated itself. As the startled Muscarello stood watching, the lights suddenly darted toward him. Muscarello dived into a ditch, and when he peered back over the edge of his hiding place, the lights were dropping down behind a line of trees as if landing in the field beyond.

Red Lights

Bertrand drove Muscarello back to the site of his encounter. The pair got out of the parked patrol car and looked about. There was nothing to be seen, so Bertrand radioed back that all

seemed quiet. Towland suggested that the field where the lights were seen to land should be investigated. Bertrand switched on his flashlight and began advancing. He was about 50 ft (15 m) from the car when cattle at the nearby farm began to call loudly as if in alarm, then mill about in excitement. Suddenly, according to Bertrand, the red lights rose up from the ground behind the trees.

Bertrand drew his pistol and Muscarello began shouting, "Shoot it, shoot it!" But as the lights came closer Bertrand thought better of opening fire and instead raced back to the patrol car. The two men hid behind the car as the lights approached to within about 100 ft (30 m). So bright were the lights, claimed Bertrand, that he began to fear that he might get burned. He scrabbled inside his car for the radio and called for backup.

Patrolman David Hunt took the radio call at 2:55 am. By the time he arrived at Bertrand's parked car the red lights had retreated. Hunt claimed he saw them clearly enough about half a mile (800 m) away. A minute or two later the lights rose higher into the sky and headed off in a southeasterly direction, accelerating rapidly as they went. All three men were considerably shaken by the experience. When word got out

As the lights approached, Patrolman Bertrand drew his gun. However – and perhaps fortunately – he did not open fire.

they came in for a fair degree of teasing from colleagues and friends, but both Hunt and Bertrand felt that they should make a formal report. They each wrote signed statements and sent these to Project Blue Book.

Was It a Flight of Military Aircraft?

The local press took up the story, prompting the Pentagon to issue a dismissive statement that the men must have mistaken a flight of B47 military aircraft that were flying over the area at the time. Bertrand and Hunt were indignant at the suggestion. Both men had spent long hours driving the lonely highways at night when aircraft of all types were flying about overhead. They felt that they knew what a B47 looked and sounded like, as well as other aircraft, and were adamant that what they had seen that night was entirely different. Moreover, Bertrand had spent some years in the USAF before joining the police and was accustomed to seeing aircraft under all sorts of conditions. In any case the B47 flight had passed over at around 1:30 am, and the sighting had continued until past 3 am. The two men wrote to Project Blue Book restating the facts and demanding that the USAF formally absolve them of making the story up or of being incompetent witnesses, a charge that might well damage their careers. After some

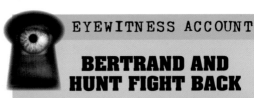

EYEWITNESS ACCOUNT

BERTRAND AND HUNT FIGHT BACK

In response to the Pentagon's explanation of the Exeter Incident, Bertrand wrote a letter to Project Blue Book in which he stated: "As you can imagine, we have been the subject of considerable ridicule since the Pentagon released its "final evaluation" of our sighting of September 3, 1965. In other words, both Patrolman Hunt and myself saw this object at close range, checked it out with each other, confirmed and reconfirmed that it was not any type of conventional aircraft ... and went to considerable trouble to confirm that the weather was clear, there was no wind ... and that what we were seeing was in no way a military or civilian aircraft." Project Blue Book did not respond to the letter, and on December 29, 1965 – nearly four months after the sighting – Bertrand and Hunt sent another letter to Blue Book in which they wrote that the object they observed "was absolutely silent with no rush of air from jets or chopper blades whatsoever. And it did not have any wings or tail ... it lit up the entire field, and two nearby houses turned completely red."

weeks, and the sending of a second letter, the two policemen received the reply they wanted. The sighting had been reclassified by Blue Book as "unidentified" and the competence of the officers accepted.

DANGEROUS GAMES

UFO encounters can be disturbing, even terrifying, but they are rarely deadly. The Mantell incident remains one of the few instances in recent history where a reported UFO sighting has resulted in a human death. Nevertheless, there have been several occasions – usually airborne incidents involving pilots – where those involved have experienced real danger.

The Gorman Dogfight

One of the best documented early examples of this took place on October 1, 1948. At 9 pm, 26-year-old Lieutenant George Gorman of the Air National Guard was on a routine practice flight in an F51 fighter. He was at an altitude of about 4,500 ft (1,400 m) and approaching Fargo Airport, North Dakota, ready to land, when he claimed he spotted a light moving below him.

Gorman thought that he was looking at the tail light of another aircraft and estimated it to be about 3,500 ft (1,000 m) beneath him, flying on a roughly parallel course at around 250 mph (400 kph). Worried that another aircraft was on his landing flight path, Gorman called up Fargo air traffic control, manned by L. D. Jensen. Jensen replied that the only other aircraft in the area was a Piper Cub a safe distance to the west. Gorman looked,

and located the Cub. Looking back at the mystery light, Gorman watched as it flew over a floodlit football ground and was astonished to see that it was not attached to an aircraft but was seemingly a flying globe of light.

EYEWITNESS ACCOUNT

"I COULDN'T CATCH THE THING"

Gorman later related: "I dived after it at full speed (about 400 mph or 650 kph in an F51) but I couldn't catch the thing. I put my 51 into a sharp turn and tried to cut it off. By then we were at about 7,000 ft (2,100 m). Suddenly it made a sharp right turn and we headed straight at each other. Just when we were about to collide, I guess I lost my nerve. I went into a dive and the light passed over my canopy. Then it made a left circle about 1,000 ft (300 m) above and I gave chase again."

Alerted by Gorman, Jensen contacted Manuel Johnson in the control tower. Johnson claimed he took out his binoculars and located the light, confirming that it was not attached to an aircraft. Jensen peered into the sky and he, too, said he saw the odd light. Dr. A. Cannon and Einar Nelson in the Cub also claimed to see it, once alerted by radio to the unfolding drama.

When the mystery light turned and began a dive toward the airport, Gorman decided to act. He was, after all, in the National Guard and flying in a fighter aircraft. He decided to give chase, but could not keep pace with it. The object then made a sharp turn and began heading straight for Gorman. At the last moment, he dipped his plane and the light passed overhead.

This time, Gorman decided, he would not pull out of any collision. Indeed he was quite prepared to ram the mystery object and radioed his intention to Fargo. Jensen and Johnson had by now abandoned their tasks and were able to follow the extraordinary dogfight that followed.

Mogul spy balloons like this one were used to spy on Soviet weapons tests and were highly classified.

The UFO allegedly seen by pilot Lerdo de Tejada in 1979 had a highly dangerous – possibly even murderous – sense of mischief.

For some 20 minutes Gorman and the mystery light chased each other around the sky over Fargo. Then the intruder seemed to tire of the proceedings. The light began a steep climb. Gorman followed it up to 17,000 ft (5,200 m), but was unable to keep up. The object flew off to the northwest at high speed. Gorman landed and filed a report.

Two Red Lights

On another occasion, a UFO apparently "buzzed" a passenger jet, forcing it to make an emergency landing. The Supercaravelle twin-engined jet liner of the Spanish airline TAE was flying from Salzburg to Tenerife on November 11, 1979. The pilot, Lerdo de Tejada, claimed that at around 11 pm he saw two bright red lights off to port at about the same altitude as his own aircraft, 24,000 ft (7,500 m). As the lights gradually approached, Tejada perceived that they were fixed to a rather larger flying object.

Due to the dark sky and dark color of the object, Tejada could not get a clear idea of the thing's shape or size. Following international procedure, Tejada called up Barcelona Air Control, in whose area he was, to report that

TALE OF THE PARANORMAL

EPISODE OVER BRAZIL

Another Supercaravelle passenger jet was involved in a sighting over Brazil on May 7, 1967. The pilot and co-pilot both claimed to spot a disk-shaped aircraft ahead of them as they approached Porto Alegre. The disk was off-white in color with a row of flashing red lights around its rim. The aircraft's course would take it past the object with plenty of room to spare, but the co-pilot kept the disk in view. As the airliner drew level with it the disk began to move, falling in beside the aircraft at a distance of about 1,600 ft (500 m) and keeping pace with it. After about 20 minutes the object altered course, accelerated sharply, and disappeared into the distance.

a second aircraft was close to his. Barcelona confirmed that they had a second aircraft on their radar screens but that they could not identify it. Tejada decided to alter course to stay clear of the intruder, then return to his path toward Tenerife.

Scary Dance

As he began the turn, however, the two red lights suddenly accelerated and climbed. They were now about 2,500 ft (750 m) from the airliner and began a bizarre dance around the TAE plane. One minute they were following the airliner, the next they were immediately above it, then they swooped down below.

Tejada was by now alarmed. The strange aircraft seemed to be playing games with him, and very dangerous games at that. When the red lights swooped down into the path of the Supercaravelle, Tejada had to haul his aircraft round in a sudden, tight turn to avoid a collision.

Emergency Landing

Tejada at once radioed Air Control and demanded permission for an emergency landing at the nearest available airport. He was directed to Manises Airport in Valencia, Spain, which was alerted to the approach of not only the jet but also the unidentified intruder. The TAE aircraft was followed to the airport by the UFO. The staff at the airport claimed that as Tejada landed, they saw that it was followed down by a large craft with two red lights. Seen from the ground the UFO was estimated to be as large as a Boeing 747. Once the passenger jet was on the ground, the UFO apparently streaked away at high speed.

Mirage Gives Chase

Following the safe landing of the TAE jet at Manises, radars detected three UFOs in the vicinity, one of which passed very close to the airport runway. A Mirage F-1 was scrambled from a nearby air base. The pilot, Fernando Cámara, had to accelerate to Mach 1.4 just to keep pace with what seemed to him like a truncated cone shape displaying changing bright colors. The object then swiftly disappeared from sight.

Cámara was then informed of a new radar echo near Valencia. As he approached the second object, the fighter's electronic flight systems somehow became jammed. After an hour and a half pursuit toward Africa, the pilot ran short of fuel and was forced to return to base.

Bentwaters

Another dramatic incident took place over Suffolk, England, on the night of August 13, 1956. The action was centered around two Royal Air Force (RAF) bases that in the 1950s were leased to the USAF: RAF Bentwaters and RAF Lakenheath. What follows is a description of the events according to the witnesses who were at the two air bases that night…

At 10:55 pm the radar operator at Bentwaters picked up an unidentified aircraft approaching fast and low from the east. The pilot of a C47 transport

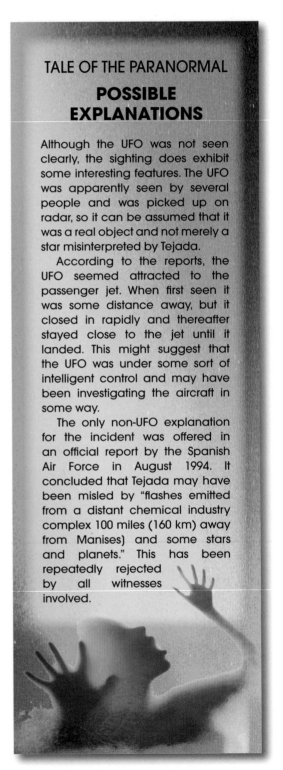

TALE OF THE PARANORMAL

POSSIBLE EXPLANATIONS

Although the UFO was not seen clearly, the sighting does exhibit some interesting features. The UFO was apparently seen by several people and was picked up on radar, so it can be assumed that it was a real object and not merely a star misinterpreted by Tejada.

According to the reports, the UFO seemed attracted to the passenger jet. When first seen it was some distance away, but it closed in rapidly and thereafter stayed close to the jet until it landed. This might suggest that the UFO was under some sort of intelligent control and may have been investigating the aircraft in some way.

The only non-UFO explanation for the incident was offered in an official report by the Spanish Air Force in August 1994. It concluded that Tejada may have been misled by "flashes emitted from a distant chemical industry complex 100 miles (160 km) away from Manises) and some stars and planets." This has been repeatedly rejected by all witnesses involved.

This dramatic re-creation shows the dogfight over RAF Bentwaters between a UFO and an RAF jet fighter.

plane that was in the area was alerted and asked if he could see anything. The pilot looked down and saw a large, soft light flash past underneath him at an estimated speed of 2,000 mph (3,200 kph). The light was seen simultaneously by ground crew at Bentwaters. Because the object was heading for Lakenheath, that air base was alerted by phone.

Soon after, Lakenheath spotted the object approaching from Bentwaters, along with two others. According to the witnesses, these three objects proceeded to perform some amazing maneuvers quite beyond the abilities of any earthly aircraft. They moved at high speed, stopped dead, and turned at right angles. Any human inside a craft turning so sharply would have been knocked unconscious and possibly killed by the forces involved.

Worried, the USAF radar operators at Lakenheath called up the RAF, which scrambled a Venom jet fighter from RAF Waterbeach to investigate. The Venom was guided toward the strange objects by ground radar, then picked them up on its air-to-air radar.

The Venom closed in to get a clear visual, but the UFO suddenly accelerated, climbed, and then dove down to get on to the tail of it. Now the hunter became the hunted as the Venom pilot threw his aircraft around in desperate attempts to get the UFO off his tail. After several seconds of fast-moving aerial action, the UFO abandoned the pursuit and took off east at high speed.

Although the Bentwaters UFO was never seen clearly, all who claimed to see it agreed that it was about the size of a fighter aircraft and glowed with a soft, pearly light that appeared fuzzy or indistinct at the edges. As with the Tejada sighting, it appeared to be controlled by some intelligence, especially during the dogfight with the Venom.

UFO Files

WHAT WAS THE BENTWATERS UFO?

The Bentwaters UFO incident was later investigated by the Condon Committee, a group set up by USAF in 1966 to study UFO sightings. The committee reported "that this is the most puzzling and unusual case in the radar-visual files. The apparently rational, intelligent behavior of the UFO suggests a mechanical device of unknown origin as the most probable explanation of this sighting." However, another investigation by aviation expert Philip Klass concluded that the incident could be explained as a combination of false radar returns and misperceptions of meteors – there were an unusually large number of shooting stars that night, associated with the Perseid meteor shower.

Bass Strait Encounter

On the evening of October 21, 1978, 20-year-old Frederick Valentich prepared to fly from Melbourne to King Island and back. His task was to collect a catch of crayfish to be served for dinner in the officers' mess of the Victoria Air Training Corps, where he was an instructor. He had made the flight many times before, but this was the first time he had done so at night. Although young, Valentich held an unrestricted pilot's license and was keen to increase his logged solo night flying time. The crayfish mission was an ideal opportunity to do so.

Valentich took off in a Cessna 182 at 6:19 pm and at 7 pm he passed over Cape Otway lighthouse. He was now flying over Bass Strait, the stretch of sea between Tasmania and mainland Australia.

At 7:06 pm Valentich radioed Melbourne Flight Control to ask if there were any other aircraft in his area. Melbourne replied that no known aircraft were around. So far as they were concerned Valentich was alone in the night sky. There was a slight pause, then Valentich reported that a

large aircraft showing four bright lights had just flown by about 1,000 ft (300 m) above him. This made the incident a "near miss" in air traffic control terms. The staff at Melbourne asked Valentich to confirm that he was reporting the close presence of a large aircraft. Valentich did so and repeated that the object had passed him at speed.

Valentich then asked Melbourne to check with the Royal Australian Air Force (RAAF) to see if they had any

Frederick Valentich encountered a mysterious craft in midair over Bass Strait.

aircraft in the area. Such things did happen, and it was clear by now that Valentich was becoming concerned. Melbourne promised to do so.

"It's Not an Aircraft"

At 7:09 pm Valentich was back on the radio. "It seems to be playing some sort of game with me," he reported. Melbourne asked him if he was still unable to identify the aircraft. "It's not an aircraft," came the surprising response. Then a harsh crackle of static cut in, making the rest of Valentich's words inaudible. When his voice came back he was saying, "It is flying past. It has a long shape. Cannot identify more than that." There was a pause, then Valentich

The lighthouse at Cape Otway, Victoria, overlooks the wild southern seas over which Frederick Valentich's aircraft vanished.

blurted out, "It's coming for me right now," followed by another pause. Valentich seemed to calm down. "I'm orbiting and the thing is orbiting on top of me. It has a green light and a sort of metallic light on the outside."

At this point Melbourne received a response from the RAAF confirming that no military aircraft were over Bass Strait. Valentich radioed to say that the strange object had vanished. All seemed well until at 7:12 pm when Valentich suddenly came back on the radio. "Engine is rough and coughing," he reported. Then a few seconds later, he said: "Unknown aircraft is now on top of me." There was then another burst of static. Then silence.

Vanished

Melbourne repeatedly tried to contact Valentich but there was no answer. King Island airfield staff were alerted to watch for the approaching Cessna. Neither sight nor sound of the aircraft was detected. At 7:28 pm Melbourne ordered that a search should begin.

Valentich had with him in the Cessna a standard life jacket and radio beacon, which was activated automatically if it fell into water. No radio signals were picked up from it. At dawn the following day the RAAF began an exhaustive search of the Bass Strait by air. A small oil slick was seen near King Island, but that could have come from any one of a dozen sources. No sign of Valentich or his Cessna was ever found.

After news of Valentich's disappearance became public, several people came forward alleging that they had witnessed unusual events in that area. Some claimed to have seen an "an erratically moving green light in the sky." Others said they saw a green light trailing Valentich's plane, which was in a steep dive at the time. UFOlogists have described these reports as significant because most were recorded before the transcripts of Valentich's final radio messages were released, when he described the object as having a green light.

UFO Files

WHAT HAPPENED TO FREDERICK VALENTICH?

Over the following weeks there were many attempts to explain what happened to Valentich. One suggestion was that he had somehow turned the aircraft upside down and was seeing the reflection of his own lights in the sea. However, he had the UFO in sight for about seven minutes and the Cessna can fly upside down for only 30 seconds before the fuel system collapses. Another suggestion is that Valentich faked the UFO sighting in order to leave his old life and start again. This is supported by the fact that no other craft was detected on radar despite the ideal conditions and the fact that Melbourne police received reports of a light aircraft making a mysterious landing not far from Cape Otway at the same time as Valentich's disappearance. UFOlogists, however, speculate that Valentich encountered a UFO and made some catastrophic error while concentrating on the UFO instead of his instruments.

THE UFOs LAND

The earliest reports of UFO sightings, and the majority of reports since, have been of flying objects seen mostly from a distance but sometimes from close up. Convincing as many people found these reports, they left behind them no evidence beyond the sightings themselves. Skeptics point out that the witnesses could have mistaken ordinary objects for something extraordinary, or that they might have been hallucinating or even lying.

Close Encounters of the Second Kind

However, during the 1950s sightings began to be reported where the UFO apparently left behind physical traces of its passing. This could be anything from car engines cutting out to more harmful effects such as the death of livestock. In the terminology adopted by UFO researchers, these are close encounters of the second kind, or

The formation of crop circles is one of the most commonly reported instances of UFOs leaving evidence of their passage.

UFO Files

WHY ARE CE2s SO USEFUL TO UFOLOGISTS?

Sightings alone, even from credible witnesses offering detailed reports, are open to all sorts of doubts. The actual size of an observed object depends very much on how far away it was when seen, and judging distances can be notoriously difficult, especially at night or when seeing an object in the air. If an object leaves physical traces, however, these can be precisely measured and analyzed at leisure. Moreover the type of traces left may indicate how the object moved, how hot it was, and of what material it was composed. For instance, holes cut from soil indicate a mechanical action, while holes burned in vegetation suggest radiant heat. They also make less likely the possibility that the witness invented or hallucinated the encounter.

CE2s. They are quite rare, but extremely valuable to UFOlogists, as they allow them to learn a lot more about the UFO phenomenon.

Engine Failure

An early CE2 that achieved widespread publicity occurred on the night of November 2, 1957, at Levelland, Texas. The fact that this took place just an hour after the Russians had launched the world's second artificial satellite probably had something to do with the publicity the incident received.

At 11 pm Patrolman A. J. Fowler answered the phone at the Levelland police station. The call was from a man named Pedro Saucedo. Fowler could tell from Saucedo's voice that he was in some distress. Saucedo reported that his truck had broken down after he saw a bright light in the sky, but that it was now working again. Unable to get many details from Saucedo and thinking the man might have been drinking, Fowler logged the call but took no action.

But Fowler was in for a busy night. About an hour after logging Saucedo's call, he took a second call from a Mr. Watkins. This caller reported seeing an object shaped like an elongated egg, about 200 ft (60 m) long, resting on the road a few miles east of Levelland. Watkins said that as he approached the strange object, his car engine had stopped and his lights had gone out. A few seconds later the object took off and headed north. The car headlights had then come on and the engine was able to restart.

Fowler had barely hung up when he received a third call from a man reporting an almost identical incident north of Levelland. A fourth call followed from a terrified truck driver northeast of Levelland. Three more calls were made the following morning, making a total of seven motor vehicles that spluttered to a stop after encountering a UFO that night.

By 1 am, Fowler had alerted all patroling police vehicles to the bizarre reports he was receiving. Patrolmen Lee Hargrove and Floyd Gavin reported a sighting of the UFO at a distance, but said it was moving too fast for them to catch it. Fire Marshal Ray Jones picked up the police radio reports and drove out to join the UFO hunt. He, too, claimed to see the UFO and, although his engine promptly spluttered, it did not stop.

Some days later, Saucedo, the original caller, and his friend, Joe Salaz, gave a rather more coherent account of what had happened to them. As they were driving west from Levelland on Route 116, they claimed they had seen a large flying object shaped rather like a torpedo coming toward them. As the object got closer their truck engine had coughed and then died, the headlights blinking out almost immediately after.

Saucedo got out of the truck to get a better look at the rapidly approaching object, which he thought was about 200 ft (60 m) long. It was, he said, pulsing with yellow and white light and giving off a tremendous amount of heat. The object passed by without pausing and headed off east. A few seconds later, the truck's headlights came back on and Saucedo was able to start the engine. He continued his journey to Whiteface, where he found a pay phone from which he made his call.

UFO Files

WHAT HAPPENED IN LEVELLAND?

After interviewing Saucedo and two other witnesses, an investigation team set up by Project Blue Book concluded that a severe electrical storm was responsible for the sightings and reported engine failures. They said a weather phenomenon known as ball lightning was probably to blame. This finding was disputed by UFO researchers at the time, including J. Allen Hynek. After examining weather records on the night in question, they have said "there was no severe thunderstorm in Levelland during the time of the sightings."

Once the local newspaper printed the story, over fifty local residents came forward to say that they had seen a strange light or object in the skies around Levelland that night.

Encounter in Tasmania

A broadly similar experience to that which befell the motorists around Levelland occurred on the evening of September 22, 1974, near Launceston, Tasmania. A woman, who preferred to be known only as Mrs. W. in press reports, drove to an out-of-town bus stop where she was due to pick up a visiting relative, parked her car by the roadside, and settled down to listen to the radio.

After a few minutes, she said, the radio began to emit a high-pitched whine. Mrs. W. reported that as she bent forward to fiddle with the radio controls she saw that the land around her car was slowly being illuminated by a whitish light. Looking up to see the source of the light the woman apparently saw a UFO approaching at a height of about 50 ft (15 m).

The object was about as big as a truck. The top half consisted of a curved dome that was pulsating with a bright orange-red light. The underside was shaped more like an inverted cone, though with distinct horizontal banding. The lower half was silvery-gray in color and was emitting a pale whitish light.

Unsurprisingly the woman decided to get away as quickly as possible. She started her engine, put the car into reverse, and accelerated away as the UFO reached within 100 ft (30 m) of her car. The car had gone barely 330 ft (100 m) when it ran off the road and the engine cut out.

UFOs are often sighted near roads. Some observers claim that their advanced technology is able to remotely override the engines of cars.

Hair Straightener

Mrs. W. watched in alarm as the UFO approached, then came to a halt. It then bobbed off to its left before climbing steeply into the sky and vanishing into clouds. As soon as the UFO was out of sight, Mrs. W. leapt from the car and ran home. Her husband met her at the door and, having calmed her down enough to get the story from her, noticed that her hair, which had been permed a few days earlier, was now straight again.

Next morning, Mr. W. walked up the road to retrieve the car with his son. They started the vehicle without trouble, but were deeply puzzled by the fact that the front half of the car was gleaming clean, while the rear half was as dirty as it had been when Mrs. W. had begun her ill-fated journey.

Somehow the UFO had not only interfered with the car radio – which apparently never again worked properly – it had also seemingly straightened Mrs. W's hair and cleaned the paintwork on her car.

Bending Beams

Rather more bizarre than simply switching them off was the effect on the headlights of a car traveling near Bendigo in Victoria, Australia, on the night of April 4, 1966. Ronald Sullivan was driving along a straight

TALE OF THE PARANORMAL

GRAVEYARD ENCOUNTER

One sighting that had a direct effect on the witness took place at Leominster in Massachusetts on March 8, 1967. A couple were driving home just after midnight when they drove past the town cemetery. They later reported seeing a light and a trail of smoke in the cemetery and stopped to investigate. The man got out of the car intending to enter the cemetery to see if something was on fire. As he did so the bright light began to rise slowly from the ground, moving silently and smoothly.

The man put out his arm to point at the rising object and called out to his wife to look. Then several things happened at once. First, the car's engine cut out, as did the headlights, radio, and dashboard lights. Secondly, the man felt a mild electric shock run through his body and his outstretched arm was pulled down to slam hard onto the roof of the car. The man tried desperately to pull his arm free, but it seemed to be glued to the vehicle.

The rising object then began to emit a loud humming sound and to rock from side to side. As the object gathered speed and moved away, the car lights came back on. The man found he could move again, and wasted no time in starting the engine and driving away as fast as he could.

Strange events at Leominster, Massachusetts, began with an eerie sighting in a graveyard.

rural road in a remote area near Bendigo when the beams sent out by the headlights of his car apparently began bending to the right.

Understandably puzzled, he braked to a halt, intending to inspect his headlights. Sullivan said that as he got out of his car, he noticed a round or domed object in a field off the road in the direction toward which the headlight beams were bending. The object was of indistinct shape and glowed with various, shifting colors, most noticeably red and blue. The object then rose into the air and flew off, after which the headlights returned to normal.

Light Display

Similarly bizarre behavior by beams of light was reported as part of a UFO sighting in France in 1972. On the evening of August 11, a group of students took part in a philosophical discussion at the open-air theater in Taizé. When the main event ended, about thirty-five youngsters stayed on for an informal meeting.

At about 2 am the proceedings were allegedly interrupted by a UFO.

According to the witnesses, the UFO was about the size of a coach and it descended out of the low clouds to hover over the shallow valley in front of the open-air theater. The object emitted a low but loud humming noise. It was dark gray, silhouetted against the yellow cornfield opposite, with a single white light at one end. After hovering

The 1972 Taizé sighting in France was unusual for the length of the time that the UFO stayed in sight – over an hour and a half.

for a while, the UFO suddenly showed seven yellow lights arranged evenly along its length. Two yellow domes then lit up on top of the UFO near to the left end. Finally, five white beams of light shone down from the underside of the UFO toward the Earth. Two quite separate UFOs then appeared, taking the form of orange-red balls of fire that hovered to the left of the main object.

Investigating the Object

It was by this time almost an hour since the dark gray mass had first appeared. Four of the youngsters – including M. F. Tantot and Mlle Renata – decided to investigate. Picking up their torches, though they could see perfectly well by the light cast from the UFO, they climbed out of the theater and began crossing the plowed fields beyond to descend into the valley over which the UFO was hovering.

It took about 20 minutes to negotiate the fence and undergrowth before they could emerge onto the valley floor. Ahead of them the four could dimly make out a large, domed object about 20 ft (6 m) tall sitting in the field. Unsure as to whether this was a harmless haystack or other object, or something linked to the UFO, Tantot switched on his torch and shone it at the object.

The beam of his torch shone straight ahead for most of the distance, but was then deflected upward as if by

UFO Files

PHYSICAL EVIDENCE?

The following morning, M. F. Tantot, accompanied by friends, returned to the scene of the encounter. In the field they found an elliptical area of dry grass 100 ft (30 m) long, approximating the length and shape of the object. In a nearby wood, in the middle of a clearing, they found a large, healthy branch lying on the ground. The part of the branch that had broken from the tree had a strange appearance. For about one-third of its diameter it looked as though it had been sawn. That portion contained an orange-colored elliptical zone that contrasted greatly with the general color of the wood. The rest of it looked as though it had been torn violently from the tree. Equally hard to explain was the color of the leaves on the branch – grayish brown and dotted with numerous small bluish-white dots. Experts were unable to say what might have caused these effects.

a mirror – though no mirror could be seen. The UFO above them then shifted its position slightly and a beam of intense white light shot out to illuminate the four youngsters beneath it. Badly dazzled, they did not see the UFO gradually lift and then shoot off at great speed, though those still in the theater saw it go. Also gone was the domed object in the field.

Glowing Sphere

If the stories are true, UFO-induced power failures do not only affect simple circuits such as those controlling car ignitions and headlights. On the evening of October 20, 1990, a much more dramatic electrical power breakdown occurred in the Botosani region of Romania.

At around 10 pm that evening Virgil Atodiresei was walking home to his farm near Flaminzi. According to his later testimony, he saw a light glowing through clouds over the nearby village of Poiana, but at first took no real notice of it. Then, so he claimed, he saw an almost spherical object descend from the clouds. It had a slightly indistinct outline, but glowed with color as if there were several bright lights moving around within an opaque globe. Atodiresei could see it was big, but could not estimate its precise size.

Meanwhile, all the lights in Poiana went out as the electrical supply failed. Power cuts in rural Romania were not unusual, so most villagers simply went to bed. However, Professor Nicolai Bildea had his students' mathematical papers to mark. He had a lantern in an outside shed and so went out into the backyard to find it. As he left his house he noticed a flickering yellow-red light. Thinking that a neighbor's barn or haystack might have caught fire despite the persistent drizzle, Bildea went out into the street to investigate.

Energy Consumer

Bildea later claimed that as he came around the corner of his house, he saw a large object shaped like a tortoise shell, about 160 ft (50 m) long and 40 ft (12 m) wide. Around the edge of the flat lower side he could see a number of small white lights. From four of these, beams of light were pointing down and sweeping the village. One swept over him briefly and was extremely bright. The rain had by now stopped, so Bildea ran back to get his wife and mother to see the UFO. By the time they reached the street the UFO was moving off and they got only a distant view of it. As the UFO left, the rain began again, this time a heavy downpour rather than the earlier drizzle. Half an hour or so later the electricity supply came back on.

UFO Files

WHAT HAPPENED TO THE ELECTRICITY SUPPLY?

The following day the villagers phoned the local electricity works, which sent an engineer out to check the systems. No faults or problems were found with the electricity supply, which was now working perfectly. Interestingly, the engineer confirmed that the flow of electricity from the local substation had continued throughout the night, rising slightly at the time the UFO was seen. It seems that something had been consuming electricity that night, but it was not the villagers of Poiana.

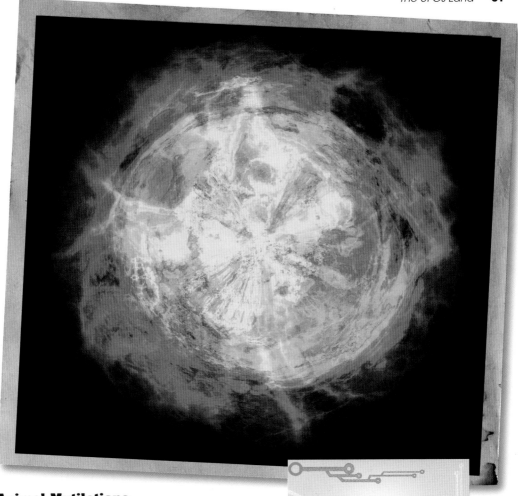

Animal Mutilations

Other physical effects have been blamed on UFOs, none more macabre than the string of animal mutilations that occurred in Alamosa, Colorado, in 1967. The apparent trail of destruction began on the evening of September 7, when Agnes King saw a fairly large, round object fly over fields near her home in Alamosa. At the time she thought little of it.

The next morning, however, Mrs. King's daughter's horse was found dead. What struck Berle Lewis, the daughter, about

UFO witnesses often report seeing glowing balls of light. Are these craft, or do they have some other, mysterious purpose?

the corpse was the fact that the head and neck had been stripped clean of flesh while the rest of the carcass was untouched. She had seen livestock killed by dogs and mountain lions, but this did not fit the way those predators ate their prey.

Some UFO researchers claim that aliens are conducting experiments on livestock. The purposes of such experiments, however, remain obscure.

The case hit the headlines and soon dozens of ranchers, farmers, and pet owners were coming forward to claim that their animals had been killed and mutilated. Many of these animal killings were not linked to UFO sightings and were probably the work of local predatory animals. Some of the more bizarre injuries were ascribed by police to disturbed people living in the area.

Diamond in the Sky

UFOs have not only been blamed for injuries to animals, but also for human injuries. On December 29, 1980, Vickie Landrum, her grandson Colby, and her employer Betty Cash were driving home from a restaurant in New Caney, Texas. They were passing through a quiet wooded area when they spotted an aircraft of some kind hovering over the trees.

According to the witnesses, the object moved to within about 180 ft (55 m), then halted and began to hover over the road in front of Cash's car. Cash braked to a halt, thinking at first that an aircraft or helicopter was in trouble and was about to land on the road. The witnesses described the UFO as shaped like a diamond, hovering with one point facing downward. It was a silvery color and seemed to glow. Around its center was a string of round blue lights. From the bottom of the craft there suddenly erupted a column of red flame, causing the object to rise slightly. When the flames cut out it sank slowly down, only to be boosted up

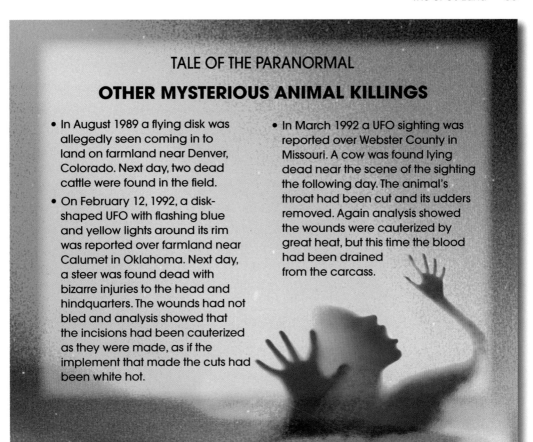

OTHER MYSTERIOUS ANIMAL KILLINGS

- In August 1989 a flying disk was allegedly seen coming in to land on farmland near Denver, Colorado. Next day, two dead cattle were found in the field.
- On February 12, 1992, a disk-shaped UFO with flashing blue and yellow lights around its rim was reported over farmland near Calumet in Oklahoma. Next day, a steer was found dead with bizarre injuries to the head and hindquarters. The wounds had not bled and analysis showed that the incisions had been cauterized as they were made, as if the implement that made the cuts had been white hot.

- In March 1992 a UFO sighting was reported over Webster County in Missouri. A cow was found lying dead near the scene of the sighting the following day. The animal's throat had been cut and its udders removed. Again analysis showed the wounds were cauterized by great heat, but this time the blood had been drained from the carcass.

again by the roaring jet. When not emitting flames, the object made a loud beeping noise.

Both Vickie Landrum and Betty Cash got out of the car to look at the object. There was a great heat emanating from it, which caused Landrum to grow uncomfortable and return to the car. After a few minutes, the object flew off. When Cash tried to open the car door, the handle was so hot that it burned her fingers. She used her jacket as a glove to open the car door. The women then saw several helicopters fly low overhead as if chasing the UFO. They watched the UFO fly off, keeping it in sight for five minutes or so, then drove home.

Sunburn

Next morning, Betty Cash woke up suffering from what appeared to be severe sunburn. She had a pounding headache and experienced vomiting attacks. Colby and Vickie Landrum also had headaches and what seemed to be sunburn, though their injuries were less severe. By mid-morning, Betty's neck had swollen up and her skin was erupting into blisters.

All three went to see the doctor, and Betty was whisked off to the hospital. She was treated for burns, but it was not until a few days later that she told hospital staff about the UFO encounter. By that time her eyes had puffed up so much that she could barely see, and her hair had begun to drop out.

The condition had eased a couple of weeks later, but recurrent attacks continued for at least two years.

Betty's eyesight never returned to normal, while Vickie became so sensitive to heat sources that she was unable to return to her work as a cook. The doctors were uncertain as to the precise nature of the injuries. Their best guess is that the three were exposed to intense ultraviolet radiation or to a burst of X-rays at high levels, though quite how this could have occurred at night on a remote Texas road remains unclear.

UFO Files

INVESTIGATING THE CASH-LANDRUM CASE

In 1998, UFO skeptic Philip J. Klass found some reasons to doubt the story. He said that in 1981 Betty's car was inspected using a Geiger counter, and no radioactivity was found. Also, no one checked the health of the three witnesses before the encounter. In response to the first point, UFOlogists say that high-energy ionizing radiation that can cause damage to human beings does not induce radioactivity in objects. A 1982 government investigation of the case found no evidence that the helicopters seen by the witnesses pursuing the object belonged to the USAF. (The helicopters were also allegedly seen by a policeman and his wife who were in the area at the time.) The investigators did, however, find Cash and Landrum to be "credible witnesses."

Stomach Burn

The Texans were not alone in sustaining injuries caused by UFOs. In May 1967 Canadian prospector Steve Michalak was investigating low-grade silver deposits near Falcon Lake, Ontario, when he came across an object in a forest clearing. The object was oval in shape and about the size of a large private aircraft. It was glowing with a vivid purple light.

Thinking that he had found some secret military aircraft, Michalak decided to investigate. Seeing what he took to be an open door, he went to have a look inside. As he approached the door, it suddenly slammed shut and shot out a stream of searingly hot vapor. Michalak's shirt burst into flames, so he tore it off as he hurriedly ran away. Heading for the nearest town, Michalak began suffering from vomiting and headaches. When he was admitted to the hospital, doctors found that his stomach had been badly burned in a neat grid-like pattern where he said he had been hit by the vapor.

Scorched Earth

In July 1969 two teenage girls reported seeing a UFO hovering low over a field. They said it was shaped like an upturned soup bowl, though with a bottom that was only slightly concave. It was colored silver and seemed to have had a band of softly glowing orange light around its rim. The girls thought that the UFO was about the size of a truck.

It made a loud whooshing noise as it climbed away from the field.

One of the girls was the daughter of the farmer who owned the field. The girls were frightened by what they had seen, but the farmer refused to believe them and sent the friend home, thinking that the girls were up to some sort of prank.

In December 1980, Vickie Landrum and Betty Cash saw a group of helicopters apparently pursuing UFOs.

TALE OF THE PARANORMAL

LANDING MARKS?

On May 11, 1969, Marcel Chaput, a Canadian log mill worker, was woken up at around 2 am by the sound of his dog barking furiously. Light was streaming in at the window. Chaput claimed he looked out and saw what seemed to be an intensely bright light hovering over a field some 600 ft (180 m) away. He threw on a coat and boots and hurried out with his dog. According to Chaput, as he emerged from the house, the light dimmed. He estimated that the bright light was about 15 ft (4.5 m) above the ground. The object then began to make a loud purring noise and rose into the air before flying off.

The following day, Chaput and his family went out to the field. They found three small circular marks as if dinner plates had been pushed hard into the soft ground. The marks were arranged in a triangle, in the center of which was a rectangular mark about 2 in (5 cm) deep. Chaput guessed that the circular marks had been made by landing legs and the rectangular mark by a hatch of some kind – though he had seen none of this the night before.

The following day the farmer looked at the field where the alleged encounter had taken place and found a large circular area where the plants looked as if they had been subjected to intense heat. The leaves and stems were wilted, browned, and, in places, dry to the touch. None of the plants had been crushed or pushed over, so whatever had affected them had not come to rest.

Disks in the Desert

On November 23, 1957, a USAF lieutenant, whose name is suppressed in the Blue Book report, was driving near Tonopah in Nevada just after dawn when his car engine suddenly cut out. The lieutenant got out to inspect the engine and heard a high-pitched whine over to his right. He claimed that when he looked around, he saw four silver disk-shaped objects sitting on the desert about 900 ft (270 m) away.

Realizing at once that he was seeing something very unusual, the officer took the time to study them. According to his description, each object was about 50 ft (15 m) across and 10 ft (3 m) tall. On top of each was a smaller dome some 5 ft (1.5 m) tall and 10 ft (3 m) across. The disks were silver in color and the domes seemed to be semitransparent, though nothing could be seen of the dome interior. Around the rims of the disks was a dark band that seemed to be rotating slowly. Underneath each

UFOs appear to have a particular affinity for the deserts of the American Midwest.

craft were three half-spheres of a dark color, which seemed to be landing gear of some kind.

Having seen all he could from the road, the officer decided to approach the objects to get a closer look. When he was about 50 ft (15 m) from the objects, the whining noise rapidly increased in pitch and volume until it began to hurt the man's ears. The

objects then lifted off the ground and swept off to the north about as fast as a man could run before eventually disappearing behind some hills.

Once the objects were gone the officer went forward to the place where they had rested. He found that each object had left three shallow marks in the ground corresponding to the landing gear he had seen. The marks were circular, about 1 in (2.5 cm) or so deep and were arranged in a triangle about 10 ft (3 m) or so along each side.

Returning to his vehicle, the officer was able to start the motor without trouble. He drove back to his base where he reported the sighting. The report was not made public at the time and emerged only after Project Blue Book closed in 1969. A note attached to the file by Blue Book staff back in 1957 reads: "The damage and embarrassment to the USAF would be incalculable if this officer allied himself to the host of "flying saucer" writers who provide the air force with countless charges and accusations.

In this instance, as matters stand, the USAF would have no effective rebuttal or evidence to disprove any unfounded charges." The sighting was officially explained as due to "psychological factors," though what they were was not recorded.

Ring of Dry Earth

One of the best documented CE2s occurred in Delphos, Kansas, in 1971. At dusk on November 2, 16-year-old Ron Johnson went out to pen his family's small flock of sheep for the night. Ron claimed that as he did so he noticed a bright light in a small clump of trees about 75 ft (23 m) from where he

Ron Johnson glimpsed a glowing object slowly rising from a copse of trees.

was walking. According to Ron, as he watched, the light rose steadily and he could make it out to be a disk-shaped object about 10 ft (3 m) in diameter with a single cylindrical support beneath its center. It was making a loud, uneven whine.

Ron raced back to his house and alerted his parents. The parents claimed they came out just in time to see the object clear the top of the trees and fly off. After waiting to see if it would return, the family nervously entered the clump of trees. They said they found that one dead tree had been knocked over, a branch had been broken off a living tree, and there was a softly glowing ring on the ground.

Next morning the Johnson family alerted the local newspaper and police. The journalists got there first. They found that the dead tree had been pushed over recently and that the broken branch seemed to have been snapped off by a heavy weight pushing down from above. Although the leaves on the branch were fresh and green, the wood itself was dry and brittle, as if it had been snapped off weeks earlier.

The place where the UFO itself had apparently landed was marked by a ring of dry soil – the rest of the earth was muddy due to heavy recent rain. The surface of the dry soil was crusted and slippery. When they dug down they found that the dryness extended for more than 1 ft (30 cm) beneath the ground surface.

When the police arrived, they confirmed the journalists' findings, and added another remark to their report: the trees near the landing site seemed to be discolored compared to others in the copse. In the weeks that followed, the Johnsons noticed that the undergrowth near the landing site was growing back. Four years later it had grown back everywhere except on the ring of soil where the alleged UFO had landed.

UFO Files

ANALYZING THE RING

The ring of earth was composed of a whitish substance, a sample of which was sent to a laboratory for analysis. The findings were as follows:
(It was resolved into fibers which) was vegetal in nature and belonged to an organism of the order of Actinomycetales, which is an intermediate organism between bacteria and fungus... family actiniomycete, genus Nocardia... (and is) often found together with a fungus of the order Basidomycetes, which may fluoresce under certain conditions... one possible interpretation is that high energy stimulation triggered the spectacular growth of the Nocardia and of an existing fungus, and caused the latter to fluoresce.

Space Agency Investigation

In 1981 a CE2 allegedly took place at Trans-en-Provence, France. The event was not particularly unusual in UFO terms, but it has acquired importance because it was investigated thoroughly by GEPAN, a department of the French Space Agency.

Nicolai Collini, an unemployed engineer, reported that he was busy in his back garden repairing a water pump at around 5 pm on January 8 when he heard an odd whistling noise. He looked up to see, so he later claimed, a dark gray object flying toward him over a pine tree on the far side of a large open field. It was spinning as it flew down at a gentle angle. He described the object as circular, shaped like two plates placed rim to rim, and about 5 ft (1.5 m) tall. There was a pronounced flange around the

French mechanic Nicolai Collini was at work on a water pump when a UFO came in to land barely 100 ft (30 m) away from him.

UFO Files

GEPAN's INVESTIGATION

GEPAN reconstructed the flight path of the UFO. They calculated that it was flying at around 21 mph (34 kph) when it was first seen and came to rest three seconds later. This, they said, would give it a deceleration of around 0.32G. On takeoff it took three seconds to clear a line of trees, giving an acceleration of 0.45G. By measuring the indentation left in the soil by the object and the load-bearing strength of the soil, the object was estimated to have weighed around 1,540 lb (700 kg). Whatever powered a craft of this weight, the estimated deceleration and acceleration rates would have needed a thrust of around 15,776 lb (7,171 kg). The soil in the indentation was dry and brittle, indicating that it had been briefly heated to a high temperature, perhaps as much as 1,112°F (600°C).

rim, he said. On the underside were four dark patches, which Collini took to be openings of some kind.

Intrigued, Collini walked over to the edge of his property to get a closer look at the object. It came down gently, coming to rest in the middle of the field about 100 ft (30 m) away from Collini. After sitting stationary for a few seconds it rose slightly, hovered briefly, then took off in the opposite direction from Collini

to clear the trees again and depart in a northeasterly direction.

Once the object had left, Collini scrambled into the field and ran to the landing site. He found a circular indentation in the soil. Around the edge were some marks, as if a sharp object had scuffed the ground. The dip in the soil was about 8 ft (2.4 m) wide and around it there was what seemed to be a ridge about 4 in (10 cm) wide.

Collini reported his sighting to the authorities and the next day men from GEPAN were on the scene. They obtained a detailed account from Collini, took measurements of the landing site, the height of the trees, the distance involved, and other matters. The final conclusion of the GEPAN team was that Monsieur Collini had witnessed an "unconventional event."

Y-Shaped Marks

On the night of March 6, 2000, a group of people allegedly saw a glowing round light swoop over their village of Kampung Gobek in Malaysia. According to the witnesses, the object seemed to hover, then dived down slowly before appearing to land in a stretch of marsh near the village. As it descended, the object sent out flashes of light as bright as, and similar to, lightning. After a few minutes, the object took off again.

The majority of crop circles have turned out to be the work of humans.

A group of more intrepid villagers went to inspect the spot where they believed the object had landed. They reported that the vegetation had been flattened over a fairly wide area and indentations left in the soft soil. The marks were "Y" shaped, measuring 50 ft (15 m) by 18 ft (5.5 m). Some 4 ft (1.2 m) from this mark was a second depression shaped like a crescent about 10 ft (3 m) across.

The Livingston UFO Assault

One of the strangest and most disturbing reports of a CE2 came from Livingston, Scotland, in 1979. When forestry worker Robert Taylor walked into a clearing in a wood outside Livingston, west of Edinburgh, on November 9, he expected to see nothing more exciting than his pet dog chasing rabbits. What he claims he did see changed his life.

It was 10 am when Taylor left his pick-up truck to walk through the dense stands of conifers. His task was to check the fences and gates surrounding the forest and ensure that no sheep from neighboring farmland had got in. His dog, an Irish setter named Lara, had run ahead of Taylor but was nowhere to be seen. Presumably it was somewhere in the forest searching for rabbits. The following is based on Taylor's account of what happened next...

In the center of the clearing was a dark gray object about 20 ft (6 m) across. It was round with a high-domed top and a narrow rim projecting out from its base. Standing up from the rim were a number of poles topped by what looked like small propellers. At intervals around the base of the dome were darker round patches that were almost black in color. The object seemed to be hovering slightly above the ground, but was emitting no noise. It was, however, giving off a strong smell akin to burning rubber.

Understandably, Taylor came to a sudden halt as he stared in some surprise and no little alarm at the object. Almost at once, he realized that he was being approached by two small round black balls that came from the direction of the gray object.

UFO Files

CROP CIRCLES AND SAUCER NESTS

In 1966, just outside Tully in Queensland, Australia, locals found an area of marsh where the reeds had been flattened in a swirling, circular pattern. Although no UFO had been seen in the area, the local press dubbed it a "saucer nest" and speculated that it had been formed by a flying saucer. Similar saucer nests turned up occasionally over the following years, but it was a group of three that appeared in wheat fields outside Westbury in Wiltshire, England, that really sparked interest in the phenomenon. Each circle was about 60 ft (18 m) in diameter. The standing wheat in the nests had been bent over close to the ground so that it lay almost flat, but the stems were neither broken nor cut. Nor was there any sign of burning. The stalks were bent down in a swirling, circular pattern, the middle of which was off-center within the circle itself. At the edge of the circle there was an abrupt change from bent stems to those standing upright. The British press dubbed them "crop circles" and suggested a link to UFOs, although none had been seen. Weather experts suggested that a relatively rare form of fair weather whirlwind was to blame. These form when warm summer sun unevenly heats up air close to hills. The rising air forms a vortex that can spin with increasing speed to reach around 100 mph (160 kph) for short periods. Given that all the crop circles formed near hills in warm weather, the meteorologists suggested that this was the cause. The general public, however, seemed to prefer a mystery.

Each ball was a little under a meter in diameter and had half a dozen straight legs sticking out from it. The balls rolled toward him on the legs, making a soft sucking noise as each leg touched the ground.

Things were happening fast. Before he could back off, the two spheres had reached him and each pushed out a leg to grab hold of his leg with another soft sucking sound. The balls began to move back toward the larger object, dragging Taylor with them. Now alarmed, Taylor struggled to get free. The burning stench increased in intensity to the point where Taylor found he could barely breathe. Gasping for air and trying to fight off the black spheres, Taylor felt himself growing dizzy and losing consciousness.

He woke up some 20 minutes later lying face down on the grass, with Lara moving about agitatedly nearby and whimpering. The strange objects had all gone. Taylor's trousers were torn where the spheres had grabbed him. One of his legs was badly bruised and his chin was cut and bleeding. He tried to stand, but his legs were weak, so he began to crawl back toward his truck. When he tried to talk to Lara, he found he could not utter a sound. Reaching the truck, Taylor tried to radio his base, but was still unable to speak. He headed home, his house being closer than the forestry base.

Marks in the Grass

When he staggered through the door, Taylor was at last able to talk. He gasped out his tale to his wife, who phoned Taylor's boss Malcolm Drummond, who in turn called a local doctor, Gordon Adams. Drummond arrived first with a team of workmen and headed into the forest to investigate.

When the men reached the clearing, they could not see anything at first. Then one of them spotted some strange marks in the grass. Drummond ordered the men out of the clearing so that they did not disturb the ground, and called in the police.

UFO Files

STUDYING THE MARKS

The police went to the clearing and examined the marks in the soil. They found two parallel tracks some 8 ft (2.5 m) long and 1 ft (30 cm) wide. These were formed of crushed grass as if an enormously heavy weight had rested on them. Around these tracks were two circles of holes driven into the soil. Each hole was circular, about 4 in (10 cm) across and 6 in (15 cm) deep. There were 40 holes in all, each of them driven down at an angle away from the tracks. Checks with forestry workers revealed that no heavy machinery had been used in the clearing for months. Police forensic checks showed nothing unusual about the soil samples taken from the holes or beneath the tracks.

Tests on the Victim

Dr. Adams arrived and examined Taylor. All the tests came up normal, though Taylor by this time had a pounding headache to add to his minor bruises and cuts. Adams suggested an X-ray, but the local hospital was too busy and by the time the X-ray machine was available, the headache had gone, so Taylor never bothered having the test.

The police took away Taylor's clothing for forensic tests, but found nothing unusual. The tears to the trousers were consistent with them being tugged violently by blunt hooks rather than being cut. In fact, everything the police found was entirely consistent with Taylor's story. But what the object was and why it was in the forest has never been explained.

Robert Taylor was – he believes – attacked by strange, six-limbed objects of alien origin.

GLOSSARY

aerobatics Feats of spectacular flying.

altitude The height of an object in relation to sea level or ground level.

atomic bomb A bomb that gets its destructive power from the rapid release of nuclear energy, causing damage through heat, blast, and radioactivity.

ball lightning A rare and little-known kind of lightning that takes the form of a moving globe of light several inches across and can last for periods of up to a minute.

"buzz" (slang) Fly very close to (another aircraft, the ground, etc.) at a high speed.

cauterized Burned the skin or flesh (of a wound) with a heated instrument, usually to stop bleeding or prevent the wound from becoming infected.

CE1 A close encounter of the first kind is an alleged sighting of a UFO, in daylight and at close quarters.

CE2 A close encounter of the second kind is an alleged encounter with a UFO, in which the UFO leaves some kind of evidence behind, such as marks on the ground or injuries to humans or animals.

CE3 A close encounter of the third kind is an alleged encounter with a UFO, combined with the appearance of what seem to be occupants or crew from the UFO.

comet A celestial object consisting of a nucleus of ice and dust and, when near the sun, a "tail" of gas and dust particles pointing away from the sun.

conspiracy theory A belief that some covert but influential organization is responsible for an unexplained event.

credible Able to be believed; convincing.

echelon A military formation in parallel lines, with each line projecting further than the one in front.

elliptical Having a regular oval shape.

flange A projecting flat rim, collar, or rib on an object.

flap An episode during which a large number of UFO sightings are reported in a particular area.

fluoresce Shine or glow brightly.

flying saucer A popular term for "UFO."

forensic Describing the application of scientific methods and techniques to an investigation.

fuselage The main body of an aircraft.

Geiger counter A device for measuring radioactivity.

hallucination An experience involving the apparent perception of something not present.

harvest moon The full moon that is seen nearest to the time of the autumnal equinox.

inverted Upside down.

landing gear The undercarriage of an aircraft, including the wheels.

Mach the ratio of the speed of a body to the speed of sound. So Mach 1 is the speed of sound, Mach 2 is twice the speed of sound, etc.

maneuvers Movements requiring skill and care.

meteorite A meteor that survives its passage through the Earth's atmosphere and strikes the ground.

meteors Small bodies of matter from outer space that enter the Earth's atmosphere and appear as streaks of light.

mirage An optical illusion caused by atmospheric conditions.

opaque Not transparent.

Perseid meteor shower A meteor shower occurs when a number of meteors appear to radiate from one point in the sky at a particular date each year. The Perseid meteor shower is the annual shower of meteors that appears to radiate from the Perseids constellation.

phenomena (plural of phenomenon) Facts or situations that are observed to exist or happen.

pipe clay A fine white clay used especially for making tobacco pipes.

port The side of a ship or aircraft that is on the left when one is facing forward.

Project Blue Book A systematic study of UFOs conducted by the USAF, which ran from 1952 until 1969.

protrusion Something that extends beyond or above a surface.

pulsate A regular, rhythmic brightening and dimming.

radioactivity Energy emitted in the form of particles by substances such as uranium and plutonium, whose atoms are not stable and are spontaneously decaying.

scramble Order (a fighter aircraft) to take off immediately in an emergency.

Soviet Union A former federation of communist republics that occupied the northern half of Asia and part of eastern Europe between 1922 and 1991. After World War II it emerged as a superpower that rivaled the USA and led to the Cold War.

supersonic A speed greater than that of sound.

truncated Shortened by cutting off the top or the end.

UFO Unidentified flying object – a mysterious object seen in the sky for which, it is claimed, no scientific explanation can be found.

UFOlogist A person who studies UFOs.

ultraviolet (of radiation) Having a wavelength shorter than that of the violet end of the visible spectrum, but longer than that of X-rays.

undulating Moving with a smooth, wavelike motion.

USAF United States Air Force.

vegetal Of or relating to plants.

weather balloon A balloon equipped with special equipment that is sent into the atmosphere to provide information about the weather.

FURTHER INFORMATION

Aliens and UFOs, by Christopher Evans (Carlton Books, 2008).

UFO's: Alien Abductions and Close Encounters (Graphic Mysteries), by Gary Jeffrey (Book House, 2006).

UFOs and Aliens: Investigating Extraterrestrial Visitors (Extreme!), by Paul Mason (A & C Black, 2010).

UFOs (Trailblazers), by David Orme (Ransom Publishing, 2006).

The Mystery of UFOs (Can Science Solve…?), by Chris Oxlade (Heinemann Library, 2006).

UFOs and Aliens (Amazing Mysteries), by Anne Rooney (Franklin Watts, 2009).

Web Sites

Due to the changing nature of Internet links, Rosen Publishing has developed an online list of Web sites related to the subject of this book. This site is updated regularly. Please use this link to access the list:

http://www.rosenlinks.com/pfiles/ufos

INDEX